DATE DUE

BROWNSON ON DEMOCRACY
AND THE
TREND TOWARD SOCIALISM

Brownson On Democracy And The Trend Toward Socialism

BY
LAWRENCE ROEMER

PHILOSOPHICAL LIBRARY
NEW YORK

Andrew S. Thomas Memorial Library
MORRIS HARVEY COLLEGE, CHARLESTON, W. VA.
45899

Copyright, 1953, by the
PHILOSOPHICAL LIBRARY, INC.
15 East 40th Street, New York 16, N. Y.

PRINTED IN THE UNITED STATES OF AMERICA

To my benefactors, particularly Father William
J. Bergin, C. S. V., and the John J. Maddens.

CONTENTS

Chapter		Page
	Acknowledgments	ix
	Introduction	xi
I.	Brownson the Man	1
II.	The Origin of Government in Contract	19
III.	The Democratic Theory	31
IV.	The Nature and Origin of Political Authority	49
V.	The Nature of the State	65
VI.	The Union of States	82
VII.	The American Republic	96
VIII.	Democracy and the Destruction of American Institutions	116
IX.	Conclusion	146
	References to Introduction	153
	References to Chapter 1	154
	References to Chapter 2	158
	References to Chapter 3	159
	References to Chapter 4	162
	References to Chapter 5	164
	References to Chapter 6	167
	References to Chapter 7	169
	Index	171

ACKNOWLEDGMENTS

The author is grateful to those at De Paul whose encouragement and assistance rendered possible the publication of this work. It includes ideas presented originally in a doctoral dissertation in Loyola University's graduate school of philosophy. The advice of Dr. Charles J. O'Neil who directed the dissertation and Dr. Beatrice B. Roemer was most helpful. Dr. Paul Kiniery, Dr. James Anderson, Fathers Paul Kennedy, S. J., M. A. Feltz, C. M., and James A. Lowney, C. S. V., contributed suggestions, comments and criticisms, some of which are incorporated in the present work. The author also wishes to thank Mr. Arthur M. Schlesinger, Jr., for permission to publish passages from *Orestes A. Brownson; A Pilgrim's Progress,* published by Little, Brown Co. in Boston, 1939, and the Macmillan Co. for permission to quote from *Orestes Brownson Yankee, Radical, Catholic* by Theodore Maynard.

INTRODUCTION

THE WORLD is divided into hostile camps. The sharp conflict which exists between East and West extends also to the realm of ideas. Thus the international spotlight is focused upon the political principles of the two most powerful representatives of conflicting ways of life, the United States and Russia.

Both nations proclaim themselves champions of democracy and defenders of freedom, but their concepts obviously differ. Zealous and patriotic Americans ridicule Russian interpretations and endeavor to clarify the distinctively American meanings of democracy and freedom.

Unfortunately the deeply antagonistic attitudes which exist tend inevitably to arouse intense emotional rather than rational responses. Consequently the loyalty of our spokesmen is frequently more commendable than their powers of analysis. Patriotism is of course a virtue, but not one that can be divorced from reason. Waving the flag on the fourth of July, whether literally or rhetorically, is not sufficient to distinguish Russian from American democracy. If the task were so easy because of the intrinsic absurdity of communism, no educated man would assent to its principles. This is of course contrary to fact. Graduates of our most respectable universities have been convicted as communists.

Furthermore if education and communism were mutually exclusive our intellectual fortresses would automatically become bulwarks against communism. There would therefore be no need to guard them so vigilantly against

INTRODUCTION

communistic influences. The fact that communism has appealed to intellectuals and that intellectual institutions are scrutinized so carefully would indicate that communism is logical rather than illogical.

To imply that communism may be logical means simply that it follows as a conclusion from certain premises; that it is consistent with its own principles; that no laws of logic are violated when it draws its conclusions from the principles with which it begins. If communism is consistent with its own principles we are required either to accept its conclusions or to challenge its premises.

Many Americans have endeavored to ridicule the logic of communism. More than a century ago an American acknowledged as one of the greatest masters of applied logic in his day tried desperately to discover a flaw in the communistic analysis. James Russell Lowell commented on the strength of his logic:

> The worst of it is, that his logic's so strong,
> That of two sides he commonly chooses the wrong;
> If there *is* only one, why he'll split it in two,
> And first pummel this half, then that, black and blue.

This man, Orestes Brownson, could not split communism in two, nor could he beat it black and blue. That Brownson understood communism and its logic, as well as the principles from which it proceeds, is rather evident because he himself formulated its conclusions more than a decade prior to the publication of the Communist Manifesto, and independently of any contact with Marx.

Brownson endeavored to demonstrate that a trend toward communism was beginning everywhere in the world. Despite contemporary ridicule and protest to the contrary he maintained that such a trend was beginning to develop in America. He recognized it as potential, as a germ which would continue to grow unless eradicated.

The trend which Brownson recognized more than a

INTRODUCTION

century ago is now so apparent that few if any political philosophers deny its existence even in America. Unfortunately few if any recognize as clearly as Brownson the ideas responsible for its existence.

Brownson's analysis of the principles whose acceptance renders communism inevitable is rather startling, because it is contrary to an idea so familiar that we accept it without investigation. This familiar idea is democracy.

The exposition which follows presents the clear, simple and unequivocal arguments which prove that the principles producing communism are the same principles ordinarily labelled Democratic. These are the principles formulated and accepted by the majority of Americans. To accept them and to draw anything other than ultra-socialistic conclusions is to be irrational. The arguments which substantiate this important conclusion must be understood rather than dismissed as absurd simply because they are unfamiliar.

Brownson recognized communism as the most deadly enemy of both freedom and American institutions. Yet the communistic conclusion is irrefutable if the democratic premises he accepted were true. Consequently he devoted a large part of his life to an intensive study of democratic principles and to the foundation of American institutions.

In his careful analysis of the American republic Brownson discovered certain elements designed to guard against the centralization of power and its abuse. These elements are distinctively American. They are found nowhere else in the world. Their preservation is necessary for the continued existence of our institutions.

Brownson's exposition of the basic nature of our republic differs from traditional interpretations which restate the position of either Webster or Calhoun. In point of fact the possibility of transcending their expositions is rarely suggested today.

This seems rather strange since neither Webster nor Calhoun claimed infallibility. Their arguments, originally

INTRODUCTION

formulated to prove a thesis, are based upon a particular philosophy, which may of course be wrong. It is therefore neither arrogant nor impertinent for Brownson to suggest that it is unscholarly and imprudent to assume that the views of Webster and Calhoun are in any way exhaustive or ultimate.

The point at issue is not that a masterful logician proves that both of these men were wrong. This is inconsequential, save as a scholarly footnote in a learned exposition.

The fact remains that their theories concern an existing reality, the American republic, which is responsible for establishing and maintaining for individuals the largest liberty they have ever known. Neither Webster's nor Calhoun's versions expose those distinctively American elements whose preservation is essential for the continued existence of liberty. This viewpoint is also contrary to opinions generally accepted, but again it is necessary to understand the evidence substantiating the conclusion before dismissing it.

This brief introduction has suggested that Brownson was acknowledged by his contemporaries as a master logician, and that his arguments were presented clearly, simply and conclusively. In view of these facts it seems rather strange that his political principles have been neglected.

The explanation is not to be sought in his lack of popularity. He and his review were known to most of the influential men in America. Comparatively recent biographies by Arthur Schlesinger, Jr., Theodore Maynard and Doran Whalen were circulated extensively. Articles about him still appear rather regularly, particularly in Catholic journals.

Brownson's political principles are neglected primarily because he himself mislead his biographers and commentators. He stated that his only systematic exposition on government, which he called *The American Republic,* contained his best as well as his final and definitive thought

INTRODUCTION

on political problems. It was as a matter of fact neither his last nor his best work.

The *American Republic* cannot possibly be the best that Brownson wrote. In order to produce it Brownson, already an old man, attempted to divest himself of his temperament and disposition as well as the habits and training acquired throughout a lifetime as a reviewer. This is a work in which he professes to quarrel with no one. Consequently the Brownson who won the admiration and the respect of his contemporaries because he wrote with such power and precision as a controversialist is conspicuous by his absence in the *American Republic*. The work is therefore nothing more than a convenient summary for those already familiar with Brownson, and a curious and confusing collection of conclusions unsupported by evidence for those unfamiliar with his essays.

Nevertheless, in discussing his political principles Brownson's biographers seldom if ever go beyond his *American Republic,* which is rather embarrassing for both Brownson and his biographers. Mr. Maynard, for example, stating that his point of departure is a summary of the *American Republic,* repeats the view that it is Brownson's best book (p. 326) ; he adds that it is a pity that it has been neglected because written by a Catholic (pp. 340-345). It is somewhat surprising then to see that in the opinion of the same critic a large part of the book is devoted to the refutation of a thesis that no sensible man has ever doubted, that its theses are compressed and disconnected logically and that the latter part of the work is unrelated to the first.

One wonders at the outset why an author as distinguished as Mr. Maynard is concerned with someone whose life was devoted to the refutation of a thesis no sensible man ever doubts. But if the work is deserving of such criticism it is an obvious abuse of common sense to recommend it as Brownson's best. It proves rather that Brownson is unbecoming in author's garb.

INTRODUCTION

It would seem that a simple recognition of the fact that Brownson's *American Republic* has little value is the first requisite for sustaining the interest in the life and work of Brownson aroused partially by the biography of Mr. Schlesinger.[1] The work disturbed one of the many Brownson enthusiasts, Sr. Mary Rose Gertrude Whalen, C.S.C., who wrote her own version of his life and work.[1] The Catholic World featured as an article a very harsh review of the work by the Rev. Wilfred Parsons, S. J.[1] Mr. Maynard, dissatisfied with the works of both Schlesinger and Whalen, attempted to supply the omissions of both and to correct inaccuracies, particularly in the study of Whalen.[1]

The present work is an exposition of Brownson's political principles emphasizing particularly the argumentation whereby he supports his conclusions. This task requires one to sift the pertinent material from the multitude of articles on political topics penned by this prolific writer from 1838 to 1875.[2]

Orestes Brownson was a professional reviewer. As such he touched upon every important issue in his day. In his commentaries he strove to analyze his subjects carefully, to delve into the basic principles involved. So it is that in his observations on contemporary problems he frequently transcended immediate issues to enter the realm of philosophy.

Since Brownson's discussions were prompted by current issues, it is difficult to comprehend and to evaluate his political philosophy without noting specifically the problems that prompted it. Detailed biographical information, however, is not pertinent to the topic treated, and is furthermore unnecessary because of the comparatively recent biographies already cited. Therefore it seems advisable to begin with a survey of the salient features of his life and times, selecting information that is helpful, and even necessary, for an understanding of Brownson's position.

1

BROWNSON THE MAN

ORESTES A. BROWNSON was born in Stockbridge, Vermont, on September 16, 1803.¹ His parents were Sylvester and Relief Metcalf Brownson. Sylvester died shortly after the birth of Orestes and his twin, Daphne Augusta. The boy was one of six children. When he was six years old his mother, unable to continue the support of her family, placed Orestes with an aged couple in the town of Royalton where he was reared.

The people with whom he lived were New England Congregationalists.² Brownson says that they treated him with great kindness and affection. However, he led a rather isolated existence:

> Properly speaking I had no childhood . . . Brought up with old people, and debarred from all the sports, play, and amusements of children, I had the manners, the tone, and tastes of an old man before I was a boy. A sad misfortune.³

Because of his environment Brownson was free to devote a great part of his time to reading, an accomplishment he achieved at an early age. He read whatever was available, although this was comparatively little. He was interested particularly in the Scriptures and especially in the Passion. Thus he says that his reading was confined ". . . principally to the Scriptures, all of which I had read before I was eight, and a great part of which I knew by heart before I was fourteen years old."⁴

He recounts an incident at the age of nine which gives us an insight into the temperament which characterized both his youth and maturity. He tells us that he was permitted to accompany a much older boy to the square at Royalton —

> ... to witness a muster, or general training of a brigade of militia. On returning home, I was asked what I had seen to interest me. I answered that I had seen two old men talking on religion. In fact, I was so much interested in their discussion that I quite forgot the soldiers, though I came of a military family, and almost forgot to eat my card of gingerbread. The discussion, I remember, was on free-will and election, and I actually took part in it, stoutly maintaining free-will against Edwards, who confounds volition with judgment . . .⁵

This incident indicates that Brownson possessed a rather unusual aptitude for becoming involved in arguments. He mentions also that he possessed this inclination in common with a fiery temper: "I had an irritable temper, and was subject to violent outbreaks of passion, but I tried hard to control myself, . . . and, till I was man grown, I do not believe I ever suffered the sun to go down upon my wrath."⁶ The incident indicates further the primacy which matters pertaining to religion and controversy occupied in the life of Brownson. In fact anything as mundane as a card of gingerbread remained of secondary importance throughout his life.⁷

As has been noted, Brownson refers to his lack of childhood companionship as a sad misfortune. While it undoubtedly was such in the sense that it deprived him of something, it also encouraged his tendency to meditate upon scriptural passages, and especially upon the accounts of the Passion.

And while his solitude was due in part to circumstances over which he had no control, it was also partially voluntary. Thus he says:

> Sometimes I seemed to hold long familiar conversations with him (Christ) and was deeply pained when anything occurred to interrupt them. Sometimes, also I seemed to hold a spiritual intercourse with the Blessed Mary, and with the holy angel Gabriel, who had announced to her that she was to be the mother of the Redeemer. I was rarely less alone than when alone . . . I preferred to be alone, for then I could taste the sweets of silent meditation, and feel that I was in the presence of Jesus and Mary, and the holy angels; yet I had not been baptized, and had very little instruction except such as I had obtained from reading the Holy Scriptures.[8]

While Brownson had no particular instruction in religion he frequently attended the meetings of the various sects which were held in the vicinity. These included the Methodists, Baptists, Universalists and Christians. He could discover no difference in their respective doctrines, but he preferred the Methodist preachers because they

> . . . appeared to have the stronger lungs; they preached in a louder tone, and when they preached the people shouted more. I thought them the best, because they made the most noise, and gave the most vivid pictures of hell-fire, and the tortures of the damned. All I learned, however, from either was, that I must be born again or go to hell, get religion or be damned. The more I listened to them, the more I feared hell, and the less I loved God.[9]

At the age of fourteen he left his guardians. His mother took him, along with the rest of the family, to Ballston Spa, in New York. He earned his livelihood by working in a printer's office. He also attended an academy in the vicinity, but only for a very brief period.[10] His stay at the academy marked the beginning and end of his formal education. During this period he retained his interest in religion, but he was exposed to many conflicting theories. He encountered atheists, Universalists, deists. His mind became confused. The more he trusted his reason, the further it led him from religion. Yet he felt the need of religion. He was in a position which necessitated a choice between reason and religion.[11] At the age of nineteen he decided in favor of religion. He says that he was passing a Presbyterian meeting house on a pleasant September day, entered it, and was deeply affected by the services. The following Sunday he was baptized and received as a member of the congregation.[12]

His life as a Presbyterian was not very agreeable. After attending his first meeting on the day after his baptism, he realized he had made a mistake. The account of his "Presbyterian Experience" in *The Convert* describes the particular congregation he joined.[13] It also describes his own repugnance towards Presbyterianism and its doctrines.[14] His position was a painful one. He endured his torments for two years. During this time he analyzed his position. He had abandoned reason for an authoritative teacher. In Presbyterianism he found no authority. It directed him to the Bible, asking him to read it with a prayerful mind. Thus it disclaimed all responsibility as an authoritative teacher. Brownson immediately detected an unfairness in this attitude:

> But while the Church refused to take the responsibility of telling me what doctrine I must believe, while she sent me to the bible and private judgment, she yet claimed authority to condemn and excommunicate me as a heretic if I departed from the standard of doctrine contained in her confession.[15]

Having become more keenly aware of his position, Brownson realized very vividly that he had made a mistake in abandoning his reason. For if he denied it, or looked upon it as unworthy of his confidence, he would be as though he were without it. Consequently he would be no better than an ox or an ass. Therefore he would be qualified no better than an ox or an ass to determine whether God exists or has made a revelation. Furthermore, an ass could not receive a revelation even on the supposition that God exists and has made one. So he decided that to revoke reason as he had done was a "cowardly act, the act of an intellectual desperado."[16] Hereafter he would trust his reason. He would never again abandon it. He would not believe anything which contradicted it. Brownson made this decision at the age of twenty-one. He says of it that it marks the beginning of his intellectual life.[17]

After severing connections with Presbyterianism Brownson also left New York in order to teach at Detroit. Some time after arriving there he became a victim of malaria. He was so seriously ill that he was not expected to recover. He was confined to his room during the latter part of 1821 and the early part of the following year.[18] During his illness he turned his attention toward Universalism.[19] After his recovery he returned to Vermont. He applied for and received a letter of fellowship as a preacher, and was formally ordained an Evangelist during the summer of 1826.[20]

Following his ordination Brownson returned to New York. He lived and preached successively in Fort Anne, Whitehall, Litchfield, Ithaca, Geneva and Auburn.[21] This period of his career is important for two reasons: In 1827 he married Sally Healy. It also marks the beginning of his career as a writer. He wrote articles for *The Gospel Advocate and Impartial Investigator,* and became its editor in 1828. Brownson describes his connection with the magazine:

> I had written a good deal for the periodical while at Ithaca, had charge of it during the absence of its

editor, and had acquired through its pages considerable reputation as a writer ... I conducted it for a year, but with more credit to my free, bold and crude thinking, than to my piety or orthodoxy even as a universalist.[22]

Brownson soon became dissatisfied with Universalism. It was unreasonable. Somewhat untactfully for a minister he expressed his doubts openly, not only in regard to Universalism but in regard to Christianity. He and Universalism were incompatible. His own brief description is again cited as indicative of the temperament characteristic of Brownson.

But with these doubts hanging over me, it was clear that I could not, as an honest man, present myself before the public as a Christian minister. It is true I did not write or preach differently from what I thought and felt ...

But, although I was beginning to acquire a prominent position in the denomination, I felt that I ought to leave it. I could not consent to profess what I did not honestly believe ...

I wanted the truth, would labor for it, harder than most men perhaps, but never to stop with its mere apprehension or barren contemplation. My disposition was practical rather than speculative.[23]

This somewhat detailed exposition of his early life indicates Brownson as a man who was impulsive, as evidenced by his sudden entrance into Presbyterianism. Once in a position he examined it very carefully. Thus he developed a power of analysis — of stripping an issue of anything extrinsic. In Presbyterianism he wanted an authoritative teacher; he did not find it. Anything else was merely embellishment. Brownson was interested in one issue at one time: i.e., in concentrating upon one side of it to the exclusion of everything not explicitly *ad rem.*

As a writer and a lecturer he was, as indicated, bold and free; he was also crude in the sense that he lacked subtlety or polish. He had a fiery temper. He was imprudent in his utterances, having little regard for the consequences ensuing from what he said. He loved truth. He wanted to convey it to others, to defend it against any and all comers. As a man writing boldly and writing to defend his stands he was presented with innumerable occasions for developing his talents as a controversialist.

This brusque, independent individual continued his search for truth after abandoning Universalism. He became attached to many movements for reform, such as that of Robert Dale Owen. He preached and wrote as an independent minister, became a Unitarian minister, and was associated with the Transcendentalists. His account of these experiences is given in his *Convert,* and is also stated in some detail in the biographies already cited.

In his search for truth he read what may be referred to conveniently as the ordinary works on religious and philosophical questions in which he was interested. Being reared among Protestants, and not having encountered the works of the scholastics, he read, among others, the works of Locke, Reid, Berkeley, Hume and Godwin. Quite naturally he was influenced by the men he read.[24] Some of the philosophers famous in the day were French. With the help of a dictionary Brownson was able to read the works of Pierre Leroux and Victor Cousin, both of whom confessedly influenced him a great deal.[25] While Brownson was by no means an accomplished linguist, he was able to acquire a knowledge of several other languages, including German, Spanish and Italian. The most prominent of the Germans, Kant, and later the Italian, Gioberti, also influenced Brownson.[26]

Now it has been noted that these men influenced Brownson. The way in which they influenced him indicates, as exactly as that is possible, the nature of the man whose political philosophy is to be investigated, as well as the terms in which his thought is expressed.

It seems that Brownson accepted, for example, the views of Leroux and Gioberti,[27] in much the same way that he accepted Presbyterianism. He was always desperate for truth. He accepted very eagerly whatever these men said that seemed to him to be reasonable. Having accepted it, he would analyze his position carefully. Usually he found that something they said was true, at least in some sense, and something was false. The truth must be retained and the error rejected.

Having investigated these men, absorbed what they said, Brownson adopted their terminology. He says, for example, that the formula of Gioberti, *Ens Creat Existentias*, IS true confessedly not as Gioberti holds it, but as Brownson holds it.[28] He said the same thing in regard to Leroux's doctrine of communion — that man lives by communing with his fellow man. What both of these men said is false, according to Brownson, but it is not false if properly understood. Nothing is more true than the fact that God created all things, and nothing is more true than the fact that God created man so that he needs the society of his fellow man in order to develop his capacities.

Having accepted such views eagerly, and having been accustomed to analyzing them rather zealously he accepted their terminology and used it. Thus the Brownson who is writing, lecturing and attempting social reforms of one kind and another, is a man who has accepted truth from a great many sources, expressing it in somewhat unusual terms.

In the course of his career Brownson founded a magazine of his own in order to be unhampered in his expression by editorial restrictions. This magazine he called the *Boston Quarterly Review*. He used it as an organ for expressing whatever he thought ought to be said and also for supporting the Democratic party, which he thought would secure necessary reforms. He expressed his thoughts boldly, vigorously, clearly. His views attracted considerable attention. The Democrats rewarded his efforts by giving him a political position. He came to be regarded as a leader in the Democratic party.

In 1838 Brownson was a Democrat in the sense that he was a member of that party, which he supported in his *Quarterly Review*.[29] He was also a Democrat in the sense that he accepted as true the popular conception of democracy, which in his estimation meant to ". . . assert equality as a natural right, and to assume . . . that the introduction and maintenance of equality between man and man is desirable, and essential to the moral, intellectual, and physical well-being of mankind on earth."[30]

Having accepted the democratic principle of equality as a good theory, Brownson also had the courage to try to secure its practical realization. Thus he says that "I had had the incredible folly of treating the equality asserted as if it meant something, as if it could be made a reality, instead of a miserable sham."[31] For that reason he published in his review an essay on the laboring classes.[32] It appeared in 1840, during the presidential campaign of that year. In it he argued that it is nothing short of an absurdity to prate piously of equal rights unless the mights as well as the rights of men are equal.[33] So he advocated, among other things, the destruction of great business corporations, the modern credit system, and urged also the modification of the factory system and suggested that the denial of the right to inherit property would tend to equalize men's rights.[34]

Brownson gained much notoriety by his publication and subsequent defense of his "Essay on the Laboring Classes." When he published it he was connected with the Democratic party, and it was as a leader of that party that his views were received.³⁵ The opposing party therefore reprinted the essay and circulated it as widely as possible to indicate that these were the views of his party.³⁶

The appearance of Brownson's "Essay on the Laboring Classes" and the election of 1840, mark the end of his career as a politician, and the beginning of his career as a political philosopher. Because he published his essay, the Democratic party lost faith in him; because the ". . . people sold their birthright for a barrel of cider," Brownson lost faith in popular democracy:

> The famous election of that year wrought a much greater revolution in us than in the government . . . We for one confess — and we care not who knows it — that what we saw during the presidential election of 1840 shook, nay, gave to the winds all our remaining confidence in the popular democratic doctrines.³⁷

Since Brownson received a practical demonstration of the fact that he must revise his views, he began to re-examine his position. He contended both at this time and later that his reasoning was sound. However radical his conclusions seemed, they were not only consistent with, but the only ones derivable from, the premises given to him by his countrymen.³⁸

Having found no fault with his reasoning, Brownson began to re-examine his premises. He became keenly aware of the fact that he must have a philosophical foundation in order to take an intelligible stand in his comments on current events. Consequently he investigated more carefully questions concerning the origin and ground of government. It is at this time that the influence of Plato is discernible.

Rather remarkable is the fact that Brownson discovered that he lacked an element without which he could not speak intelligibly of authority and liberty — this was an infallible authority to determine whether or not freedom is real freedom and not license, and authority is not despotism. Thus Brownson defended, prior to his conversion and without a knowledge of the writings of Catholic philosophers and theologians, the view that government cannot be sustained without infallible authority.[39]

Since his political views were based upon what may be referred to as unique synthesis of ideas gathered from the various sources mentioned, Brownson's political position is merely a concrete illustration of the inconsistency of his general position — that he accepted and defended infallible authority without investigating the claims of the only institution which claimed to be infallible. Brownson was the first to recognize this inconsistency. Yet, he tells us in his autobiography that if he investigated this institution and if it required him to reject the doctrines which brought him thus far, and which he knew to be true, he would have no reason for seeking admission to the church. With some hesitation, therefore, he sought an interview with the Bishop of Boston. Describing his decision to seek such an interview, he says:

> It was, no doubt, unpleasant to take such a step, but to be eternally damned would, after all, be a great deal unpleasanter. Accordingly, with fear and trembling, and yet with firmness of purpose, in the last week of May, 1844, I sought an interview with the late Right Reverend Benedict Joseph Fenwick . . . and in the following week, visited him again, avowed my wish to become a Catholic, and begged him to be so kind as to introduce me to some one who would take the trouble to instruct me, and prepare me for reception, if found worthy, into the communion of the church. He immediately introduced me to his coadjutor, who has succeeded him, the Right Reverend John Bernard Fitzpatrick.[40]

Brownson's description of his interviews with Bishop Fitzpatrick represented his most tactful writing. There was no meeting of minds. The doctrines Brownson held must be waived; ". . . but, if I rejected or waived it, what reason had I for regarding the church as authoritative . . . or for recognizing any authority in the Bishop himself to teach me?"[41]

Thus Brownson writes that it was two or three months before there was any indication that they would ever come to an understanding. He could not indicate his difficulty.

> . . . lest the Catholic Bishop himself should deprive me of all reason for becoming a Catholic, and send me back into the world utterly naked and destitute. I had made up my mind that the church was my last plank of safety, that it was communion with the church or death. I must be a Catholic, and yet could not and would not be one blindly. I had gone it blind once, and had lost all, and would not do so again. My trouble was great and the Bishop could not relieve me, for I dared not disclose to him its source.[42]

However, Brownson notes that he and the Bishop soon came to a good understanding, without discussing at all the merits of his own views. He was baptized and confirmed on Sunday, October 20, 1844.

As a Catholic Brownson continued his career as a reviewer. He founded *Brownson's Quarterly Review*. With the approbation of his bishop, he continued to write on religious and philosophical matters, usually on the occasion of reviewing a book that dealt with such matters.

Politically, his views did not change a great deal. Brownson did not try to prove that a good Catholic could also be a good American citizen. He stated boldly and simply that no one can be a good American citizen unless he is a Catholic. He maintained from the start that Catholicity is necessary for the republic, and that it cannot exist without it. Thus an article in his review for October, 1845, is entitled,

"Catholicity Necessary to Sustain Popular Liberty."[43]

This brief survey of what Brownson did immediately after his conversion is given to indicate that there was no complete and radical break in the trend of his thought subsequent to his conversion. Yet, as has been indicated, Brownson was compelled to adopt an entirely new approach to these subjects. Thus one might say that it was by request that Brownson procured another dictionary and began, at the age of about forty-one, to study the works of St. Thomas and St. Augustine. Consequently he shifted also the ground and the terms in which his new arguments were formulated. Therefore those subscribers who had been following the trend of his thought could see no connection whatsoever between the Brownson who wrote before and the Brownson who wrote immediately after his conversion. It was not until some years later that he returned to his own doctrine of communion.[44]

At the time Brownson was converted, he was at the peak of his popularity. His essay on the laboring classes had been circulated by the hundreds of thousands. He appealed to the kind of audience that the Catholic journals at that time did not reach. The continuation of his *Review* was therefore desirable. "The bishop told him that he should not hide his light under a bushel, upon which Van Wyck Brooks' comment is, "as well urge a bull not to pretend to be a lamb."[45]

The following paragraphs indicate effectively Brownson's attitude immediately after his conversion:

> We have no occasion to stop to defend ourselves or our church . . . The false charges against Catholics can do us no harm, unless we suffer them to frighten us and induce us to stop and repel them . . .
>
> We must attack the enemy's camp, and arraign Protestantism herself. She, not the church, is the question; she, not the church must be put on the defensive . . . We must drag her from her covert,

force her into the light, and compel her to stand and make her defense.

Our duty calls us to act on the offensive, to expose the sorceress, to show what it is that has bewitched our brethren and holds them spellbound. Protestantism is strong only when she is suffered to attack and keep Catholics on their defense. Attacked herself, she is as tow at the touch of fire.[46]

Being somewhat belligerent about his position, Brownson suffered no one to insult the Faith. Anyone attacking the Church in a vulgar or derogatory manner did so, in the presence of Brownson, at the risk of incurring bodily harm. His son cites an instance, also referred to by Maynard, in which a man called Hoover insulted the Church: "Brownson simply took hold of him by the coat collar and the seat of his trousers and tossed him over the stove."[47]

Brownson, as is evident, took his religion seriously. He and his review made an impression. The review itself attracted considerable attention. Not only did it enjoy rather wide circulation in the United States but it was also reprinted in England.[48] As a Catholic reviewer Brownson was seldom critical of persons. He invariably endeavored to praise the person while criticizing the product of his pen. Somewhat naively, Brownson was unable to understand why such an attitude should make him the target of antipathy.[49]

Devoting his efforts to detecting errors in the works of others, and subsequently defending his judgments, Brownson continued to develop his talents as a controversialist. He abhorred inconsistency. Finding it in the work of another he expressed his repugnance graphically — almost cruelly.

This means, of course, that while Brownson invariably silenced an opponent, he did not thereby gain acceptance for his own viewpoint. It means that few people would be willing to argue a point with him. Rather than cite testimonials to that effect, of which there are many, it is perhaps more effective to cite an instance of Brownson's glee in encountering one whose avowed purpose was to carry on a series of arguments with him. After commenting that Protestantism is an unintellectual religion, and that Protestants have made a sorry figure of reasoning on religious questions, Brownson writes:

> It is, therefore, refreshing to meet even one Protestant who shows some signs of intellectual life, who has the courage to make some show of argument, and who, perhaps, has understanding enough of the matters on which he writes to be capable of being refuted. We had well-nigh despaired of ever meeting such a one, and now that he presents himself we greet him cordially and cherish him as a friend. We hope his courage will not fail him at the first onset, and that he will not as soon as he receives the first blow, like our ordinary adversaries, disappear, to be seen or heard of no more for ever. Seriously, it gives us pleasure to meet a Protestant who has a beard on his face, and who has the strength to give and take sturdy blows. We are tired of combatting mere boys or mere *simulacra*, or shadows as unsubstantial as the ghosts of superstition.[50]

While Brownson's writings may be characterized as direct, hard hitting, blunt, forceful, it is not true that he is entirely impersonal. It is not at all unusual to find him disrobing in public. In the midst of an argument it is rather ordinary for him to introduce purely personal matters, for example, in discussing the enfranchisement of women, Brownson says that "Even her tongue is a weapon that is more effectual than a man's fist, as Lucretia Mott, the Quakeress preacher, proved to us personally some years ago at the tea-table of one of her nieces."[51]

The Brownson described thus far has been a man who is

bold, rough, independent and somewhat ruthless as a controversialist. His temperament and profession were not the kind conducive to congenial personal relationships. As a layman writing a Catholic review, Brownson's position necessitated personal contact with members of the hierarchy. Quite obviously, difficulties developed; they may be described briefly as personal rather than doctrinal. For example, Brownson wrote an essay on "Archbishop Hughes on Slavery."[52] The archbishop had opposed Brownson's attitude on the question. In defending himself Brownson adopted a procedure typical in his reviews. He is mystified by the language of the archbishop, for his words indicate that he has undoubtedly incurred excommunication.[53] Brownson, however, refuses to believe that the illustrious prelate has really meant to separate himself from the church. "All the presumptions are that, both as a Catholic and a man, he agrees with the church . . ." Consequently he concludes that "We can accept no such interpretation of his language, and even if we were unable to explain it away, we would still insist that he did not and could not mean it, and should wait with our confidence in him unimpaired till he should see proper to favor us or the public with his own explanation."[54]

This is cited as an instance of the logic-chopping which, while in this and many other instances was confessedly irrefutable, did not help Brownson's position. Whether through the influence of Archbishop Hughes or some one else in an authoritative position whom he offended in a similar way, Brownson's *Review* was delated to Rome for examination. Somewhat gleefully, Brownson announces, in an article entitled "The Church not a Despotism," that Rome, while somewhat puzzled by certain things, could find nothing contrary to faith in what he said.[55]

Some time later, however, Brownson apologized very humbly for his general attitude:

I must myself confess, to my shame and deep sorrow

that for four or five years, ending in 1864, I listened with too much respect to those liberal or liberalizing Catholics ... My faith was firm, and my confidence in the church unshaken, but I yielded to what seemed at the moment a wise and desirable policy.[56]

During this period of his life Brownson's political views altered radically. Almost to the outbreak of the civil war, he had taken the position of Calhoun in commenting upon practical problems.[57] In the period immediately preceding the civil war, Brownson found himself defending the Union. In order to maintain his position consistently he was obliged to investigate more carefully the nature of the Union. The results of his investigations are embodied in his work entitled *The American Republic.*[58]

Brownson's book was motivated primarily by patriotism. He believed sincerely that American republicanism preserves certain inherent characteristics which represent the reason why America has secured for the individual the greatest liberty man has ever known. Brownson endeavored to transcend immediate issues and to expose its essential elements. In doing so he believed he was contributing to the welfare of the republic.

During this same period, ill health, along with other factors such as harsh and imprudent attacks upon individuals and institutions[59] and his support of Fremont for president necessitated the discontinuance of his review in 1864. From that time until 1872, when his wife died, he wrote[60] for Catholic periodicals, particularly the *Catholic World.*

Mrs. Brownson, realizing that her husband was too independent to submit cheerfully to editorial revisions and restrictions (especially those of one who was formerly his devoted follower, Isaac Hecker of the *Catholic World*) requested on her death bed that her husband revive his *Review*. In order to gratify her wish, as well as to prove to the public that he was, and had always been, devoted to the

Church, Brownson's *Review* appeared again in January of 1873. In October of 1875 ill health again required him to cease its publication. In his valedictory[61] Brownson says that it is only with considerable pain that he can grasp a pen. He makes his final profession of faith and expresses gratitude to those who supported him during the thirty-one years he had appeared before them as a Catholic reviewer. He indicates also that he will continue to labor for the Church despite the discontinuance of his *Review*.

Appropriately, perhaps, Brownson argued to the last. In his final controversy, Brownson's son was unable to see the force of his father's logic. After retiring to his room, Brownson replied to a knock on his door: "If that's you, Francis, I'm too tired to make it any plainer tonight."[62] He died on April 17, 1876. He is buried in a crypt, in the center aisle of the University Chapel at Notre Dame.

2

THE ORIGIN OF GOVERNMENT IN CONTRACT

THAT government derives its just powers from the consent of the governed is enumerated among the self-evident truths in the Declaration of Independence. Consequently the idea that consent renders a government legitimate is familiar to most Americans and is accepted without reservation. In many instances indeed this concept serves as a foundation for expositions which emphasize the democratic character of our own political organizations.

Brownson too commences his discussion of American institutions with this concept. But unlike most of his contemporaries and too many of his successors he refused to acknowledge this theory as a final pronouncement of truth. On the contrary he deemed it advisable to examine the theory rather critically. For if this view of government and its authority is unsound the popular accounts of our institutions which assume its truth are defective.

The theory which derives government from the consent of the governed is obviously concerned with the rightfulness of government rather than its origin as a fact. The king of Great Britain, for example, had the power to govern his colonies in America, but he did so without consulting their will. His government was therefore declared to be tyrannical and the revolt against it morally just. The view expressed in the Declaration of Independence means then that lawful authority originates in the consent of the people.

Brownson endeavored to render his analysis of the theory complete. He is therefore interested in the possible interpretations of the term people. He observes that it may be used either individually or collectively. In the first case it signifies individuals as such; in the second case it signifies a group rather than individuals. The term army, for example, is applied not to each individual soldier, but to the group as such. The term people is sometimes used in the same way to signify the group rather than the individuals which constitute it.

The theory which derives the authority of government from the people has therefore two principal variants: 1) the authority of government is derived from the consent of individuals who agree or contract to establish government and to submit to its authority. This view is frequently referred to as the contract theory of government. Hobbes, Locke and Rousseau are among its most distinguished advocates. 2) The authority to govern inheres in the people considered collectively who possess it as a unit.

Brownson refers to the first of these as more properly the contract theory and we shall present his criticism in this chapter. The second, which he prefers to call the democratic theory, is presented in the chapter which follows:

Locke states rather accurately the position Brownson intends to criticize:

> Man being, as has been said, by nature all free, equal, and independent, no one can be put out of this estate and subjected to the political power of another, without his own consent. The only way whereby anyone divests himself of his natural liberty and puts on the bonds of civil society is by agreeing with other men to join and unite into a community, for their comfortable, safe, and peaceable living one amongst the other ... This any number of men may do, be-

cause it injures not the freedom of the rest; they are left as they were in the state of nature. When any number of men have so consented to make one community or government, they are thereby presently incorporated and make one body politic, wherein the majority have a right to set and conclude the rest.[1]

Since the purpose of the theory is to account for the origin of government, it must assume that civil society is not as old as man; that there existed prior to the formation of civil society a combination of circumstances necessitating a convention to institute government. Otherwise there would be no need for a theory to account for the origin of government. The situation in which men found themselves prior to a convention authorizing government is referred to as the state of nature.

In general terms the state of nature is one of continual warfare. Each man has equal rights and each tries to appropriate whatever he can. The strong oppress the weak and the cunning circumvent the simple. The will of the strongest is the only law. At length, weary of perpetual warfare, men decide to form civil society. They surrender their own natural freedom and independence in order to secure the benefits of society. Without such a surrender of rights, government has no legitimate authority.

In his analysis Brownson is concerned first of all with the state of nature which must exist, on the suppositions of the theory, prior to the formation of government. Philosophers arrive at it by mentally separating man from his existence in society.

Now Brownson argues that in making such an abstraction it should be complete; that if one insists upon abstracting individuals from society he must be careful not to remove a man already civilized, imbued with the habits, manners, customs of society, to some remote island. In order to be consistent with its purpose the theory must suppose that society is not natural, but purely artificial. There cannot be even the slightest trace of society in such a state of nature; for if there were, it would be unnecessary to institute society. The theory would account for the development or perfection of an existing society and not, as it professes to do, for its origin. Furthermore, man himself can have no natural urge, no innate tendency for society; if he had, society would be natural and man would be a social animal and consequently society would be as old as man. Therefore it would be unnecessary to account for its origin in convention.[2]

Brownson argues that in terms of an abstraction consistent with the purpose of the theory, the people in the state of nature could not institute government. In the first place, if the primitive state of man is natural to him, then civil society must be "supernatural, preternatural, or subnatural."[3]

Man is, however, limited by the nature which he has; it is inseparable from him. It is his only source of activity. Consequently he can neither divest himself of it, nor by his own unaided efforts give himself a nature other than the one he has. Thus Brownson says that "If his primitive state was his natural state, and if the political state is supernatural, preternatural, or subnatural, how passed he alone, by his own unaided powers, from the former to the latter."[4]

Furthermore, "In the alleged state of nature, as the philosophers describe it, there is no germ of civilization, and the transition to civil society would not be a development, but a complete rupture with the past, and an entire new creation."[5] In other words, it has been noted that there is not, and cannot be, present in the state of nature, a germ of social organization — not a root that could be nurtured or developed. But man is a dependent being and not a creator. He is not strictly a creator even in the intellectual order; he cannot create an idea any more than he could create a universe. Consequently it would be extremely difficult to conceive of civil society.[6]

Even supposing that some individual, unusually gifted, would conceive of civil society, it would be impossible for him to execute his conception. It is difficult to introduce reforms among people already imbued with the notions of authority and obedience. To modify already existing institutions and to adapt them to meet changing circumstances is a task that requires a great deal of time, skill and ingenuity. But the people in the state of nature have no habits of obedience, no habit of commanding one another. Consequently the introduction of government is at least a much greater achievement than the most radical modification of an existing institution. Consequently Brownson concludes that:

> When it is with the greatest difficulty that necessary reforms are introduced in old and highly civilized nations, and when it can seldom be done at all without terrible political and social convulsions, how can we suppose men without society, and knowing nothing of it, can deliberately, and, as it were, with 'malice aforethought' found society? To suppose it, would be to suppose that men in a state of nature ... are infinitely superior to the men formed under the most advanced civilization.[7]

Consequently the advocates of the theory beg the question nature assume, unconsciously, that the people living in it have the habits and traditions of a people already civilized. Consequently the advocates of the theory beg the question because they assume the existence of civil society as the condition upon which it can be instituted. He clarifies this point in the illustrations which follow.

Brownson maintains that it is obviously impossible to establish an ideal government such as that proposed by the various authors in their Utopias.[8] He contends that they

" . . . remain Utopias not solely because intrinsically absurd, though so in fact, but chiefly because they are innovations, have no support in experience, and require for their realization the modes of thought, habits, manners, character, life, which only their introduction and realization can supply."[9]

Likewise, the introduction of civilization is an innovation. It has no support in experience. It requires for its realization the things which only civilization can supply. Unless it is assumed that the people of the state of nature have the habits of a civilized people, it would be much more difficult to introduce a civil order de novo than a *Utopia* in a civilized state. Since the latter is impossible, so also is the former. Thus the advocates of the theory must beg the question; failing to do so they suppose a combination of circumstances from which it is impossible to institute government. In either case the theory fails to accomplish its purpose.

By the same fallacy the advocates of the theory assume unconsciously that government is essential to progress. For if progress were possible without it, there would be no need for the people of the state of nature to institute government. Without government people are therefore unprogressive. Consequently in picturing the people as capable of instituting government the advocates of the theory picture them as a progressive people—therefore as a people already in possession of one of the elements essential to progress, namely government.[10]

Brownson continues his objections to the contract theory on still another ground. Even supposing the state of nature and granting a convention to institute government, it is still impossible to account for the authority of government. His objections assumed what is evident, that government is authority exercised over subjects.

Now in the state of nature there is no sovereign, no

civil authority, because a convention is called for the purpose of establishing a government with authority. In other words, individuals presumably institute a government to which they are subject, which has the right to command and to exercise authority over them. But Brownson argues that individuals cannot create a sovereign, because the creator is, obviously, not subject in relation to the creature. Consequently, if government is created by individuals, individuals are sovereign and the government thus established is subject to them as creature to creator. Government is then the agent of the creature.[11]

That government must be conceived as the agent of the individual is also indicated by the manner in which government reputedly originates. The individuals who meet in convention are sovereign, and therefore free, with equal rights. Each must be sovereign in relation to the other because there is no authority above the individual to which he is subjected. In establishing a sovereign, the individual agrees to surrender some of his own sovereignty to a governor; in doing so, the governor has the right to govern because of the voluntary consent of the individual.

Now Brownson argues that the individual is obliged, on the supposition of the theory, to surrender all of his sovereignty, a part of it, or none of it, to the government. It is evident that if the first alternative is taken there is no basis for individual freedom. For if he surrenders all to society, he has no rights left. He is consequently a complete slave of society with no rights of his own which he may plead against it; he is no longer an integer, but a fraction of a whole with nothing except that which society chooses to give to him. In that case, as Brownson observes, "However unjust or oppressive the acts of the state, he has not only no redress, but not even the right to complain."[12]

Supposing the last alternative, the individual retains his sovereignty but merely delegates instead of surrenders his rights to society. Yet if he retains his complete sovereignty, then it follows that as sovereign he may revoke at his convenience the powers delegated to his agent, and government would have no authority over him. Brownson observes that this is a very convenient theory for some, because "The disaffected, the criminal, the thief the government would send to prison, or the murderer it would hang, would be very likely to revoke his consent, and refuse to permit his agent to punish him."[13] Thus it is a perversion of language as well as of common sense, to conceive of government as a mere agent of the individual with no authority except that which is given to it by the individual.

The other alternative is reputedly a *via media* between the extremes, but practically it is reduced to either one or the other of the extremes. If the individual surrenders a portion of his rights and retains some, who is to decide where the line is drawn? If the interpretation is left to the individual he can, obviously, interpret his rights to the extent that it virtually denies all authority over himself. If the government defines the rights of the individual, determines their boundaries, the individual has, practically speaking, no appeal from the decision of the government. On the supposition that the state has the sole authority to define the rights of the individual, there is no guarantee against absolutism. Thus Brownson says that "If then, we found government in compact, we either leave the individual his natural freedom, and then we have no government; or we subject the individual to the state, and then no individual liberty. Either consequence should lead us to reject the theory."[14]

Further, since the authority of government is derived from a compact, it is evident that its authority extends only to the contracting parties. For in the state of nature all men have equal rights. Consequently no one has the authority to govern another, for the supposition is that authority to govern originates in a contract. Therefore it follows that government has authority only over those whose consent has been given.[15]

Now it is apparent at once that few people actually consent to be governed. While voting may be construed as an act of assent very few people, especially in Brownson's day, could vote. Women and children, for example, were excluded. Government therefore has no rights over them, for they have entered into no compact and therefore the terms of a compact cannot bind them. Furthermore, Brownson notes also that Jefferson maintained (and he was logical in doing so) that the contract must be renewed by each generation.[16] This means that an existing government would of necessity expire with the expiration of each generation. Consequently, an existing government has no legitimate authority unless it has the free, formal, explicit consent of each individual it governs.[17]

In other words, Brownson denies that consent to an existing government may be tacitly given by continued residence in a territory. He argues that residence may be a matter of necessity. Likewise, the silence of individuals, or their lack of opposition to an existing government, may be a matter of necessity rather than formal approval. Since each individual is presumably free and equal, " . . . by what right can individuals form an agreement to which I must consent or else migrate to some strange land?"[18]

A summary of the second series of arguments shows that the origin of government in contract is incompatible with the idea of government as authority exercised over subjects. The theory is criticized on the basis of the consequences flowing from the adoption of such a theory. If individuals instituted government it would be the agent of individuals. Consequently it would not be an authority above them. This is illustrated in the manner in which individuals reputedly institute government. They must surrender either all or none of their rights. A *via media* is inadmissible because it is resolved practically into either of the extremes. Thus the theory if adopted would lead logically to anarchy or absolutism.

Furthermore, on the supposition that each individual has the right to complete freedom, equality, independence, government could extend, rightfully, only to the contracting individuals. This means that government cannot be extended to women and children, for they are deemed incapable of entering into such a contract. It means also that each individual of each succeeding generation must renew the contract; for no group of individuals has the right to negotiate a contract to which other individuals, with precisely the same rights, must either assent or move to a foreign land. In terms of the social contract theory, such power cannot be legitimate — it is not authority or the right to govern. Thus government in the sense of authority exercised over subjects cannot be derived from a contract of sovereign individuals.

Finally, Brownson objects to the social contract theory of society and government on the ground that a society resulting from a voluntary association of individuals is merely an aggregation; it can be held together by nothing stronger than the will of individuals to associate. Consequently there is nothing to prevent any number of individuals, whether the group be large or small, from withdrawing from the association and setting up a state of their own.

This conclusion follows because the individual, according to the theory, is sovereign in virtue of his manhood. Since he is a man irregardless of time or place, the individual is sovereign at any time and at any place. Consequently any three or more individuals may at any time or place call a convention and institute a government of their own, thus bidding defiance to the officers, tax-collectors and agents authorized by other and similar conventions. On what grounds is such a right denied? Certainly not because a convention of one hundred is stronger than that of merely three individuals. This would identify right and might, thereby legitimating every act of might, however oppressive it may be. In other words, however absurd it may seem, there is no authority in a state grounded on the contract theory which could prevent any three individuals from seceding, calling a convention and instituting government.[19]

In order to maintain itself, it is quite evident that government must have the right to exercise authority over all who are within a given area. Its jurisdiction must extend, not only to those who choose to acknowledge it, who assent or consent, but to those who are in a territory.

If government has such authority, it cannot be derived from a contract, voluntarily entered into by individuals who are sovereign in virtue of their manhood which they retain irregardless of time and place. If it does not have jurisdiction over a territory, government could not maintain itself because any number of sovereign individuals would be authorized, at any time or place, to call a convention and institute government. In order to avoid such an absurdity the conception that government has no power except that which it derives from the voluntary consent of individuals, must be rejected.

This final objection to the contract theory of government is in a sense similar to those previously stated. It rejects the theory because the consequences flowing from its adoption are incompatible with the conception of government as authority exercised over subjects.

It is, however, different from the other objections, inasmuch as it introduces a new element into the conception of government — that its authority must be territorial. Further, territory has not been introduced as an incidental element of government. It has been viewed as something essential, inasmuch as government cannot exist as authority over subjects unless its authority extends to all within a territory.

So much, then, for the theory which looks to men taken individually for the origin of authority and government.

There is another sense of "the people" as the origin and ground of government and its authority. We have already mentioned it. We must now turn to what Brownson calls the "democratic theory." Can the people, as a collective whole, be the source of a valid and morally binding government?

3

THE DEMOCRATIC THEORY

DEMOCRATIC theories and democratic principles have for Americans a sacred character. Brownson was no exception. Of the "principles of democracy" he himself says: "They were given me by the public sentiment of my country. I had taken them in with my mother's milk, and had never thought of inquiring whether they were tenable or not."[1]

Brownson had a too sincerely inquisitive mind to let his principles rest in this unexamined state. He inquired what people meant when they prated so piously of majority rule, of universal suffrage and eligibility, of democracy as asserting and maintaining equality as a natural right—which means "I am as good as you, if not a whit better."[2]

He inquired also whether the people would have the good sense to adopt the measures necessary to prevent universal suffrage and eligibility from being a mere hoax. He says that at one time he ". . . had had the incredible folly of treating the equality asserted as if it meant something, as if it could be made a reality, instead of a miserable sham."[3]

Both inquiries were answered in his "Essay on the Laboring Classes." He proclaimed, somewhat bluntly, that if people want equality, they must be prepared to remove heads protruding above the common level. For this Brownson says that "I was denounced in the press, from the pulpit and the rostrum. My friends shook their heads, and were very sorry that I had been so imprudent; ... The doctrines of my essay were received by my countrymen with one universal scream of horror ..."[4]

Brownson had discovered that political equality means social equality; his countrymen were not ready to adopt the measures necessary to secure it. Having received a practical demonstration of the fact that theory and reality did not conform, he reexamined his position. He contended, both at this time and later, that his reasoning was sound. His countrymen had said two and two — he had merely added and gotten four.[5]

Having found no fault with his reasoning, Brownson began to examine his premises. He defines democracy as the sovereignty of the people. Taken negatively, it may mean the denial of " . . . the king, the nobility, or the right of any one man, or any set of men, caste, or class, to rule over the people."[6] Taken positively it means the assertion " . . . of the absolute right of the people to govern, or their native, inherent, underived sovereignty."[7] In the same place he notes also that the term may be used also to designate the end of government — that it is to be administered for the good of the whole people. Brownson concedes that he is a democrat in this latter sense of the term, but in no other.

In discussing the democratic theory, the term is used in its positive sense to designate a doctrine that the people collectively or the political community, is the source and origin of the authority to govern. The objections to the theory are stated from two viewpoints. It will be shown, very briefly, that the theory itself is erroneous; more important for Brownson is the fact that, despite its error, there is a tendency to adopt it. Consequently the tendency itself must be exposed as erroneous.

In asserting that the people originate authority, it is evident that the first requisite is to determine what is meant by the term — not to define it, for that has already been done — but to limit the extension of the term. For obviously in speaking of a people the term does not include all of the inhabitants of the globe. Rather, it refers to *a* people, to the inhabitants of a more or less definite portion of the globe. This is evidently what is meant by the people who institute government.[8]

The first problem which arises, therefore, is to determine whether or not the people who reputedly institute government inhabit a clearly defined territory. The problem is a very important one. If the territory in question is undefined, it is evidently impossible to define the people who are to institute government.

Even on the supposition that an undefined people, inhabiting an undefined territory, could institute government, the government thus established would have no authority over a definite territory. Its authority would be consequently popular only, and not territorial. This, of course, is to return to the contract theory which has been rejected already.

On the other hand, if the term people signified the inhabitants of a territory that is clearly defined, the difficulties are equally serious. Then the problem is to determine by whom, and on what authority, territory is marked out and defined. The organized people cannot determine it, for the theory presumably accounts for the origin of the organized people. Thus to say that the people themselves fix their own territorial boundaries is to say that the people act as *a* people before they exist as such.[9] For the same reason government cannot mark out a definite territory; for there is no government until authorized by a people, and no people until a territory has been defined.[10]

It is therefore necessary to go outside population in order to discover what constitutes a people as such. Without that factor the people are not sovereign because they are not even a people. With that factor they are not sovereign because it is that which gives being to population as a people. Therefore a people is dependent upon it as a cause is dependent upon its effect. Consequently that factor, whatever it is, is more ultimate than the people. On either ground it is certain that people alone are not the source of authority.[11]

Furthermore, supposing a definite territory and therefore a people, it is still impossible to account for the authority of government. It cannot be accounted for on the basis of a unanimous consent of individuals, for that again is the theory that has been rejected in the preceding chapter. It cannot be asserted that the majority has the *right* to authorize government and enact laws, because it then becomes necessary to determine wherein the majority derives its right to govern. Obviously, it does not have right because it is a majority and therefore strongest. For this theory " . . . would identify right and might, and legitimate every government able to maintain itself. Every act of power, however oppressive, on this ground would be right, just."[12]

Therefore the right of the majority to govern must be grounded upon something more ultimate than its might. The only alternatives possible are that it is somehow based upon nature or is authorized by government. However, neither of these alternatives are admissible.

The nature of one man is equal to that of any other. Consequently no two men have an inherent natural right to govern a third. If the theory were asserted within such a limited sphere, it would tend to many absurdities. If no three individuals have the natural right to govern any two, why should the will of the hundred prevail over that of ninety-nine? The right of the majority cannot be a natural right.[13]

It is intelligible, however, to base the rule of the majority upon civil regulation. The political body adopts it as the most practical rule possible to secure the good of the governed. In this sense, however, the majority of the people does not institute or originate the authority of government. It supposes an authority already existing which authorizes majority rule.[14]

Thus the fundamental objection to a theory which states that a people is the source of its own authority is that it must argue in a vicious circle. For a conception of *a* people, or a community, must be that of a people united in some way, as by the occupation of a definite territory. But this is precisely the conception of the people as a nation and therefore already invested with authority.

Now Brownson has maintained consistently that few people, if any, would maintain theoretically that the people as a unit, a nation, or a society, is the source of its own authority.[15] The reason for this is that the theory, as he has stated it, asserts despotism, absolutism, or as he prefers to call it, Caesarian or Socialism. The fact that few people would maintain such theories openly is evinced sufficiently well by the reception given his own essay on the laboring classes.

The fact that the democratic theory as he has defined it involves despotism, is not difficult to establish. He has said that government is authority exercised over subjects. Considering it strictly, and from the viewpoint in which it is authority, its authority is unlimited. For in relation to that which restrains or limits its authority in any way, government is obviously not the authority, but the subject. Therefore government, so far as it is government and nothing else, is that which is sovereign. The search for the origin of authority is therefore the search for the sovereign.[16]

Further, the right of the sovereign to command admits of no limitations whatsoever, for inasmuch as a sovereign is limited he is not sovereign, but subject. Since he has the right to command, his subjects have the duty to obey. Therefore his command is the basis of all rights and duties. Man has no rights in the sense that he can plead them against the sovereign. For if he had, the sovereign would be subject in relation to those rights.[17]

Further, it has been noted that man's freedom cannot consist in freedom from law — which according to Brownson is the conception prevailing in America.[18] Rather, man's freedom consists in obedience to the law of the sovereign — freedom from all restraint, whether of conscience or anything else, is license and incompatible with government.

Therefore, if the people are sovereign, and if man's freedom consists in obedience to the sovereign, it follows that man's freedom consists in obedience to the will of the people. In case the term people is interpreted democratically, this means that the individual does not have the moral right to resist the will of the majority:

> The sovereignty, which is asserted for the people, must, then, be transferred to the ruling majority. If the people are sovereign, then the majority are sovereign; and if sovereign, the majority have . . . the absolute right to govern. If the majority have the absolute right to govern, it is the absolute duty of the minority to obey. We who chance to be in the minority are then completely disfranchised. We are wholly at the mercy of the majority. We hold our property, our wives and children, and our lives even, at its sovereign will and pleasure. It may do by us and ours as it pleases. If it takes it into its head to make a new and arbitrary division of property, however unjust it may seem, we shall not only be impotent to resist, but we shall not have the right of the wretched to complain. Conscience will be no shield. The authority of the absolute sovereign extends to spiritual matters, as well as to temporal. The creed the majority is pleased to impose, the minority must in all meekness and submission receive; and

the form of religious worship the majority is good enough to prescribe, the minority must make it a matter of conscience to observe. Whatever has been done under the most absolute monarchy or the most lawless aristocracy, may be reenacted under a pure democracy, and what is worse, legitimately too, if it be once laid down in principle that the majority has the absolute right to govern.[19]

But this is to disrobe democracy — it is democracy in its pristine purity. No one will accept it in its nakedness. Brownson concedes this: "We cheerfully admit that there are probably few men in the country who would, in general thesis, maintain it as we have stated it."[20]

Brownson's thesis, stated most simply, is that there is a tendency toward absolutism, existing both here and in Europe, and especially in Young Italy and Young Germany, which has not as yet been actualized.[21] He speaks of seeds of dissolution which are sown and germinated, but have not as yet attained fruition.[22] He says that even in his own day:

> Not a few of the European democrats recognize in the earth, in heaven, or in hell, no power superior to the people, and say not only people-king, but people-God . . . The people not only found the state, but also the church . . . Yet this theory is the dominant theory of the age, and is in all civilized nations advancing with apparently irresistible force.[23]

His thesis is, further, that the tendency toward absolutism or socialism or humanitarian or caesaristic democracy[24] is latent in democratic theories and principles, and is promulgated, although not avowedly so, in the promulgation of democratic principles.

His reasons as to why the theory cannot be avowed openly are plausible. In order to gain acceptance for a theory, it must be presented under the aspect of the good and the true. Falsehood as such is never embraced by the intellect, nor does the will accept anything under the aspect of evil. Consequently he says that "Socialism commends itself to the intellect of its adherents only in the respect that it is true, and to their hearts only in the respect that it is good."[25]

Therefore, for Brownson the democratic theory is so extremely dangerous because it is combined with what is good. In accepting what is good and true about it, people unwittingly accept the evil along with it. As a Catholic reviewer, he felt obliged to expose this tendency because he believed that if it were unchecked it could result only in absolutism.

The democratic tendency or theory is echoed in the dominant sentiment of the day. It is expressed in the slogans adopted by the press, and by the politicians who speak of the sovereign people, of government of the people and by the people. The people are told that democracy recognizes the equality of man, which " . . . is not displeasing when applied to those above us, but is very disgusting, unreasonable, unnatural, when applied to those below us."[26] Being equal, all men must participate equally in the administration of government. Thus democracy must secure to everyone the right to vote and to be voted for — and it must encourage reforms necessary to secure universal suffrage and eligibility.

Brownson's contention is that if these slogans are accepted and acted upon by the masses who invariably fail to say, *distinguo,* it is only a matter of time before some form of absolutism is accepted. In contending for political equality, for example, Brownson says that one must demand, in order to be consistent, social equality.[27] Theoretically, the vote of the poor man is equal to that of his more wealthy neighbor. Practically, however, the vote of an individual counts for nothing unless he casts his ballot for either of two parties.

BROWNSON ON DEMOCRACY

To organize and to control a party requires a great deal of both skill and money. Those who have neither the skill nor the money to exert influence in shaping the policies of a party are therefore not the political equals of those who are so endowed; "How pretend that you and I are equal, when you can influence a thousand votes, while I can hardly control my own, unless I have the spirit of a martyr."[28] This according to Brownson is " . . . the great and stubborn fact, which knocks in the head all your fine-spun democratic theorizing."[29]

The point is, of course, that democratic principles encourage reforms necessary to secure political equality. Having secured the privilege of voting and being voted for, it has by no means secured genuine political equality. Thus the causes which led to reforms thus far have not spent themselves; they must of necessity remain in all their force to carry the reform still further. In other words, reforms are not inaugurated to stop with a sham — agitation for equality fostered by democracy cannot stop logically at the ballot box. It must extend to society itself in order to accomplish any good that it has set out to accomplish.[30]

Since the tendency of the age is toward political, and therefore social, equality, it can stop at nothing short of its ultimate goal; complete social equality. If there is property in society, it may be distributed unequally; therefore logic demands the elimination of property. Since individuals exist, they are unequal; their continued existence is a barrier to the social equality demanded by the logic of the age. Therefore, eliminate the individual — make him not an individual, but a part of society. This is the goal of the age; whether he knows it or not, this is the aim of the humanitarian democrat:

> Yesterday he agitated for the abolition of slavery, today he agitates for negro suffrage, negro equality, and announces that when he has secured that he will agitate for female suffrage and the equality of sexes,

forgetting or ignorant that the relation of equality subsists only between individuals of the same sex; ... Having obliterated all distinction of sex in politics, in social, industrial, and domestic arrangements, he must go further still, and agitate for the equality of property. But since property, if recognized at all, will be unequally acquired and distributed, he must go further still, and agitate for the total abolition of property, as an injustice, a grievous wrong, a theft ... It is unjust that one should have what another wants, or even more than another ... Nor can our humanitarian stop there. Individuals are, and as long as there are individuals, will be unequal: some are handsomer and some are uglier, some wiser or sillier, more or less gifted, stronger or weaker, taller or shorter, stouter or thinner than others, and therefore some have natural advantages which others have not. There is inequality, therefore injustice, which can be remedied only by the abolition of all individualities, and the reduction of all individuals to the race, or humanity, in general.[31]

Commenting upon the political upheavals in Europe in 1848-1849, Brownson says that the reforms sought are basically social, not merely political: "Young Italy is socialistic; so is Young Germany; and it was its socialistic character that gave to the movement of Ronge and his associates its significance and its moderate success."[32] Even in 1849 Brownson held that the reform movement of the age can find no logical resting place short of absolutism:

> Once concede that even political equality is a good, an object worth seeking, you must concede that social equality is also a good; and social equality is necessarily the annihilation of religion, government, property, and the family. The same principles which would justify the Moderate Republicans of France

in dethroning a king would justify M. Proudhon in making war on property, declaring every rich man a robber, and seeking to exterminate the bourgeoisie, as these have already exterminated the nobility. There is no stopping-place between legitimacy — whether monarchical or republican legitimacy — and the most ultra socialism. Once in the career of political reform, — we are pledged to pursue it to its last results.[33]

While social reform culminates necessarily in the annihilation of religion, government, property and family, its success is not attained by stating such things explicitly. People would recoil from the conclusions on the ground that they are radical and destructive. Consequently with the exception of a few who are regarded as idle dreamers, the socialistic theory is not drawn to its logical consequences.[34]

Socialism is therefore presented under its aspect of good. It is developed, not merely as harmonious with Christianity, but as more Christian than organized Christianity itself. It proclaims the great truth that God has created all men free and equal. Consequently He gave equal rights to all men. He was no discriminator of persons, so obviously He did not intend possession by the few while the many are dispossessed of the good things He has created. The mal-distribution of God's creation is therefore an evil which should be remedied. Consequently socialism urges the removal of evil. In doing so it plants itself upon an apparently solid Christian foundation.

Since socialism is presented as a truth of Christianity and in its garb, Brownson says that:

> We cannot deny it without seeming to them to be warring against the best interests of society, and also against the gospel of our Lord . . . How adroitly too, it appeals to the people's envy and hatred of their superiors, and to their love of the world, without

shocking their orthodoxy or wounding their piety. Surely Satan has here, in Socialism, done his best, almost outdone himself . . .[35]

The evils pointed out by socialists are real evils. Socialism emphasizes the evil; it presents a remedy which is at once simple, understandable, appealing to men's passions while not seemingly at variance with orthodox convictions. This aspect of it gives socialism its driving force and renders it acceptable. In presenting its case socialism dwells exclusively upon physical evils. It thereby excludes moral evil. Thus it goes along with the spirit of the age, which is worldly, and whose conception of evil is restricted to physical evil. Likewise in emphasizing that good should be sought, it refers to physical or temporal good. The assumption that man's good lies in the temporal order alone is the root evil.[36]

Furthermore, socialism states axiomatically that in order to avoid evil and attain to the good, men must organize and cooperate. Being attainable through organization rather than isolated individual action, it follows that ". . . the social organization must be such as to avert equal evil from all, and to secure to each an equal share of temporal goods."[37]

The reasoning of socialism is therefore based upon an ambiguous conception of good and evil. Its advocates proceed on the assumption that there is no good other than a material good and no evil other than physical evil. However, in retaining the familiar terms, good and evil, those who have inherent convictions of moral good and evil will be deceived more easily. Failing to perceive the real purpose of the reformers, they accept their pious platitudes.

Now if man's good lies in the temporal order, there is no need for a two-fold organization to secure man's good. Consequently the Church must be rejected. Yet Christianity cannot be rejected openly:

> The Christian symbol needs a new and more Catholic interpretation, adapted to our state in universal

progress. Where the old interpretation uses the words God, church, and heaven, you must understand humanity, society, and earth; ... But while you put the human and earthly sense upon the Catholic words, be careful and retain the words themselves.[38]

In thus retaining familiar terms, people will not perceive so readily that their familiar ideas have vanished. Consequently the opposition of Christians will be neither immediate nor violent. Nevertheless, in retaining the term charity, while changing its meaning so that it signifies philanthropy, charity is no less effectually destroyed; if religion is used to signify a religion of humanity, religion is destroyed. The destruction is rendered all the more effectual because it goes on under the pretence of preserving them.[39]

In thus presenting Brownson's analysis of the socialistic tendency of his age, it is clear that he was not combatting absolute or caesaristic democracy as a reality which had attained already its fruition in America. His avowed purpose is to draw from the democratic principle of equality its ultra-socialistic conclusion. He maintains that the delusive democratic doctrine of equality fosters unrest, agitation for reform, first for political equality. Political equality requires social equality as a condition for its practical realization. This in turn is not realized completely until the individual loses his identity in the race. Having disrobed democracy, Brownson hoped that his country-men would disavow its destructive tendencies.[40]

It is abundantly clear also that in protesting against a tendency toward caesarist or absolute democracy, Brownson is not protesting against the simple idea that people should have a voice in the administration of government.[41] He is protesting against a theory which holds that the people are sovereign, and against a tendency to adopt such a theory. He has defined the people as the collective people, the political community, the state, the nation. Consequently he objects to any theory or form which leaves the popular will supreme, subject to no authority, bound by no higher law.[42] Whether the authority of the nation is exercised by one, by few, by many, is of no consequence to his argument. He says that the democratic principle of the supremacy of the people ". . . is not confined to a popularly constituted government, but is accepted and acted on by most modern governments, especially by the Sardinian, the Prussian, the Russian, and we fear also the Austrian . . ."[43]

Because of his opposition to democratic principles, Brownson also condemned the tendency toward accepting them in America. He believes that the adoption of popular democracy is a step toward political atheism, or the denial of any law above, and binding the conscience of, the will of the people as a nation.[44] In presenting his argument for this conclusion, Brownson observes that the legislators are elected by popular vote. In order to secure votes one must be popular; he is required to please at least the majority of his constituents.

Brownson contends that the easiest way to please the people is to flatter them, to defer to them, to take the law from them.[45] To flatter them, the candidate for office must appeal to the wisdom and virtue of the people, telling them also that they are sovereign. As a subject the candidate avows his intention to ascertain, and to bow to, the will of his sovereign. Having been imbued with the idea that they are sovereign, that their will must be obeyed, the people repeat to the legislator, ". . . remember your accountability to the people."[46]

It is rather a grievous offence for a candidate to oppose popular opinion. The penalty for the crime is removal from office. Consequently there is, according to Brownson, an insidious circle inherent in the nature of the democratic form. Appeals, both in terms of the people to the legislator, and the legislator to the people, are, and must be, primarily popular. It is nearly impossible to get outside of the circle of popularity and appeal to justice, truth, right, as a basis for legislative action: "If you repeat always to your statesmen 'remember your accountability to the *people*,' you must expect them to ask always, not, what is right? but, what is popular?"[47]

For this reason Brownson says that "In practice, democracy will assume but one meaning — a meaning which has passed into the axiom, 'The majority *must* rule;' which again is always practically translated, 'The majority have a *right* to rule.' "[48]

In this way the will of the people, popular opinion, is the criterion which determines whether or not a legislator should support a measure. Consequently he seldom, if ever, supports or opposes a measure because it is right or just. Such factors cannot enter into an argument, because it is assumed that the majority have the right to rule.

This, for Brownson, evinces the fact that the people collectively, as a political people, are adopting political atheism. For truth, justice, right, the moral law above the will of the people is not recognized and appealed to either by the legislator who prates of his obedience to the will of his majesty who put him in office, or by the people who, having been told that they are sovereign, demand only that the legislator remain subservient to their will and to no other.[49]

Thus Brownson contends that democracy does not beget just habits of mind. It is not, as a system, conducive to the development of the virtues necessary to sustain its existence. On the contrary he says that:

> It creates a multitude of demagogues, pretending a world of love for the *dear* people, lauding the people's virtues, magnifying their sovereignty, and with mock humility, professing their readiness ever to bow to the will of the majority. It tends to make public men lax in their morals, hypocritical in their conduct; and it paves the way for gross bribery and corruption. It generates a habit of appealing on nearly

all occasions, from truth and justice, wisdom and virtue, to the force of numbers, and virtually sinks the man in the brute. It destroys manliness of character, independence of thought and action, and makes one weak, vacillating, — a time-server and a coward. It perverts inquiry from its legitimate objects, and asks, when it concerns a candidate for office, not, who is the most honest, the most capable? but, who will command the most votes? and, when it concerns a measure of policy, not what is just? what is for the public good? but, what can the majority be induced to support? Now, as men, as friends to good morals, we cannot assent to a doctrine which not only has this tendency, but which declares this tendency legitimate.[50]

Having adopted public opinion as a criterion for the morality of statesmen, Brownson believes that it is only a matter of time before it is adopted, almost universally, as an ethical standard for individual action. If the phrase, "Everyone wants it," will justify the action of a legislator, why is it wrong for the individual to justify his action by the phrase, "Everyone does it?"[51]

Popular democracy tends to create an atmosphere in which even the individual is required to guide his activity by public opinion. What the people will do, say, or think about what he does becomes a criterion of what may or may not be done. The standard of morality, popular opinion, is material rather than spiritual. Consistently with that criterion of morality, material well-being is the sign of respectability. There is a universal struggle to acquire riches as a means of equality. Not a few are induced to live beyond their means to make a show of wealth which they have not, in order to be equal.[52]

The tendency toward popular democracy is, then, a tendency toward political atheism. It involves a materialistic standard of morality. It tends to recognize, practically, no right above the popular will. This, then, is Brownson's conclusion:

> No man can attentively study our political history and analyze with some care our popular institutions, but must perceive and admit that our state contains the seeds of its own dissolution, and seeds which have already begun to germinate. Unless the tendency we have thus far obeyed can be arrested, and a stronger and more conservative principle be brought in to our relief, all hopes of a successful issue must be abandoned.[53]

Stated briefly and simply, the democratic theory of government and authority asserts the absolute, underived sovereignty of the people collectively. In its nakedness it is repugnant; Brownson has therefore endeavored to show that *The Democracy,* clad in the apparently appealing garb of political equality and the right of the majority to rule, conceals the despotism. Phrases like majority rule and political equality evoke an emotional response and consequently are not subjected to rational analysis by the multitude.

As a Catholic reviewer, Brownson could not approve of the tendency of statesmen to accept popular opinion, with the consequent rejection of the moral law, as the standard of right. Of the "democratic politician" who professes to defer to nothing other than popular opinion, Brownson said:

> No man has so much confidence in the people; no man has so deep, so ardent a love for the hard-handed and sun-burnt-faced many; none so ready and willing to defer to the wishes, the opinions, the instincts, the will of the masses. He has no interest, no opinion, no will of his own; he is one of the people, and knows only one thing, to serve the people by merg-

ing his feelings, wishes, interests, and convictions to theirs. Find a man who so professes, and you find one you may set down to be Satan attempting to disguise himself as an angel of light.[54]

Rejecting the spiritual, there is no alternative but to substitute the material. On a materialistic basis, good and evil can mean only one thing: material possessions or a lack of them. Reforms to secure equal good for equal individuals, fostered by the democratic doctrine of equality, may attempt, on this basis, to secure the good expressed by the term political equality. For Brownson, individuals, unequal socially, are not transformed into equal political powers by the mere possession of a ballot. Consequently a genuine reform for political equality finds no logical resting place at the ballot box. Its resting place is a society in which the individual is a fraction rather than an integer.

4

THE NATURE AND ORIGIN OF POLITICAL AUTHORITY

BROWNSON presents his doctrine of the nature and location of political authority before proceeding to a discussion of its origin. He sets forth his view rather clearly, although, somewhat circuitously, in his *American Republic,* where he pursues his discussion of authority in terms of its historical origin.[1] He proceeds by stating the patriarchal theory of government. He says that it endeavors to account for political authority by tracing its development in the evolution of the family into the tribe and nation.[2] It may be viewed either as an attempt to determine the origin of government as an historical fact or as a theory which accounts for the moral rightness of civil government.[3]

In his criticism of the theory Brownson concedes that it is a true explanation of government if the question is confined solely to its historical origin. For the family, Adam and Eve, is the first society. As it grows the family expands into a tribe and finally into a nation. Thus Brownson says that the transition from the family to the tribe is ". . . natural and easy, as also from the tribe into the nation."[4] Just as all society is derived from the family so also is government. It has been noted already that government exists whenever society exists. Consequently it is obvious that government begins with the family.

Having thus accepted the patriarchal theory as stating

a truth which is more or less obvious, Brownson proceeds to criticise it as an attempt to account for the authority of government. In order to present his criticism accurately, it is necessary to state briefly Brownson's position before advancing the line of argument with which he justifies it.

Brownson maintains that a society invested with political authority is radically distinct as an entity from the family. Consequently it cannot be developed from the family by a process of direct growth or simple evolution. He tells us that if there is nothing but mere growth and expansion, the family develops into a barbarous tribe or nation. Thus he says that "With barbarians the authority of the patriarch is developed simply by way of explication; in civilized states it is developed by way of transformation."[5] Repeating substantially the same opinion Brownson says that the direct development of the family results not in a civilized state, ". . . but gives us barbarism or what is called oriental despotism."[6]

Brownson's interpretation of the terms barbarism and despotism are indicated in his criticism of the patriarchal theory as an attempt to account for the authority of government. In commenting upon the development of parental authority, Brownson observes first of all that the authority of the family is vested in the father who is its natural head. Being in possession of authority in his family the father may as a fact continue to exercise it with the growth and expansion of his family. Thus he may become chief of a tribe or king of a nation.

Now Brownson argues that the mere fact that a father continues to exercise authority in becoming chief or king, is not in itself sufficient to render that authority legitimate.[7] This is obvious because rights consequent upon fatherhood are legitimate only within the limited sphere of immediate parental relationship. Because he may govern his own children, it does not follow that a parent has the right to govern anyone else, or any children of others. Therefore if the father retains his authority to govern in the expanded family, something other than the mere fact itself is required obviously to legitimate it.[8] Consequently it may be concluded at the outset that political authority cannot be deduced or evolved from parental authority.

Thus Brownson argues that the patriarch has no inherent right to govern in virtue of the fact that he is a patriarch. His conclusion does not depend upon the way in which patriarchal authority is exercised. For if he has no right to govern others, the patriarch has no authority to govern them leniently or affectionately. In order to legitimate his government it is therefore necessary to go outside of the family itself.

Having dismissed the patriarchal theory as a basis of the moral rightness of civil government, Brownson proceeds to analyze the political system based upon patriarchal authority with a view to determining its essential element.[9] His view has been indicated to some extent for he has maintained that the distinctive characteristic of authority in regard to the family is the fact that it inheres in the father as a natural right. Transferred to the state, this means that the ruler possesses political authority as his own personal right.[10] Possessing authority as a personal right, the ruler may exercise it accordingly. Thus its exercise depends upon the pleasure of the person possessing it. It is therefore arbitrary. Thus the way in which the ruler exercises his authority is accidental; his government may or may not be tempered with affection. Consequently the essential characteristic of a patriarchal government is the fact that authority inheres in the individual as a personal right, thus giving him the opportunity to exercise it arbitrarily.

In other words, Brownson's argument is based upon the fact that authority is exercised in the same way that it exists. To the extent that authority exists as the right of an individual, he may use his own authority according to his own pleasure. This is despotism. In view of the fact that the patriarchal system is based upon the principle that political authority may inhere in an individual as his personal right or privilege, Brownson maintains that it is despotic in principle.

Now Brownson refers to any government based upon the conception of authority as a personal right as a barbaric government.[11] In using the term to designate a certain type of political organization Brownson denies that its radical meaning is "Foreign, wild, fierce" as Webster indicates.[12] He argues that foreign cannot be its primitive meaning because the Greeks did not refer to every foreigner as a barbarian. Furthermore, some of the nations which they designated by the term were rather cultured and refined, having made considerable progress in science and in art. Consequently the terms wild and fierce cannot signify the essence of barbarism. Since the primary meaning of the term is at least dubious it may be conjectured, according to Brownson, that the Greeks used the term in a political sense to ". . . designate a social order in which the state was not developed, and in which the nation was personal, not territorial, and authority was held as private right."[13] Having used the term barbarian or barbarous to signify a political order that is patriarchal in character, thus using them synonymously, Brownson says that the essence of barbarism consists in the fact that authority is privately owned.

Brownson argues further that barbarism and civilization are opposed to one another. Therefore the essential characteristic of the civil order is the direct opposite of the barbaric order. Thus the essence of the civil order is the fact that political authority is a public trust instead of a right privately owned. This is signified very appropriately by the term *res publica*, which means, in regard to authority, that it is public rather than private.[14]

Now in order to make authority a public affair, it is not sufficient to say that it is invested in the population as a whole rather than in one individual. In the nature of things no man has the authority to govern another as a natural right. Consequently no group of men, merely because they are men, however great their number may be, have in and of themselves the authority to govern any other man. The reason for this is that all men are naturally equal. Consequently to give any one man authority over another by reason of his nature, is to assert the natural inequality of men. Therefore if authority is the right of a population merely because they are persons, authority is still personal. It cannot be converted into a public trust merely by referring it to a whole population as persons or private individuals, ". . . for what is private, particular in its nature, is not and cannot be general."[15]

There is no recourse, therefore, but to go outside of people as population in order to discover the characteristic which makes it possible to conceive of authority as a public trust rather than a private right. This factor, Brownson says, is territory.[16] It was introduced as an essential characteristic of authority in the political order of Greece and Rome. In Rome full political rights were possessed only by those who occupied ". . . the sacred territory of the city which has been surveyed and marked by the god Terminus."[17] Thus its political order was organized on a territorial, rather than on a purely personal, basis. Political rights pertained not to the population as people, but to persons belonging to a clearly defined territory.[18] Territory is thus introduced as the factor which determines who has political authority. Thus in Rome the state and its authority is no longer personal. It is based upon territory. According to Brownson the introduction of the territorial element marks the passage from ". . . the economical order to the political, from the barbaric to the civil constitution of society, or from barbarism to civilization."[19]

In other words, Brownson argues that if there is no common or public territory, then there is and can be only that which is personal and therefore private. Consequently if there is authority in a system that has no *res publica,* it must be on a personal and therefore private basis. It is not rendered less personal by increasing the number of persons. If authority is personal, it cannot be public. In order to make it public, it must be based upon a *res publica,* a commonwealth. Therefore political authority represented by the state must have a territorial basis.

Territory and population are therefore mutually dependent in Brownson's theory of political authority. Without territory there could be no *res publica,* and consequently no republic. Without a state or a people there could be no public to inhabit it. Thus territory is an essential element of political authority because it defines the republic in which authority inheres. Thus Brownson says:

> The state is territorial, not personal, and is constituted by *public,* not by *private* wealth, and is always *res publica* or commonwealth, in distinction from despotism or monarchy in its oriental sense, which is founded on private wealth, or which assumes that the authority to govern, or sovereignty, is the private estate of the sovereign. All power is a domain, but there is no domain without a dominus or lord. In oriental monarchies the dominus is the monarch; in republics it is the public or people fixed to the soil or territory, that is, the people in their territorial and not in their personal or genealogical relation.[20]

Being thus organized on a territorial basis, the state and its authority is in its very nature a public thing, for political authority exists only in the republic. Existing only in this way its activity is limited accordingly. From a negative viewpoint this means that the authority of the state cannot be exercised as the private right of an individual or group because it does not inhere in them in this way. Thus the barbaric or despotic element of the state is eliminated. Positively, it means that the authority of the state, by whomsoever exercised, must be exercised in the name of the republic and for its welfare. Thus the ruler may act only as a representative or an agent of the state because it is only in this capacity that he possesses authority. Consequently in lodging authority only in the republic and therefore viewing it as public, Brownson believes that he is constituting it on a *principle* which obliges the state to exercise its authority only for the public welfare.[21]

In presenting his view of the nature and location of political authority Brownson has used the terms barbarism and despotism to signify a political system in which the nation, and its authority, is personal. He has used the term republic to signify the civil order or the state whose political order is based upon a *res publica,* which *is territory.* Thus its authority is public rather than private. Summarizing his meaning of these terms Brownson says:

> *Monarchy* and *Republic* are terms often vaguely and loosely used. All governments that have at their head a king or emperor are usually called, by even respectable writers, monarchies, and those that have not are usually called republic, whether democratic like ancient Athens, aristocratic like Venice prior to her suppression by General Bonaparte, or representative like the United States. But this distinction is not philosophical or exact. All governments, properly speaking, in which the sovereign is held to vest in the people or political community, and the king or emperor hold from the community or represents the majesty of the state, are republican, as was imperial Rome or is imperial France; all governments, on the other hand, in which the sovereignty vests not in the political community, but in the individual and is held as a personal right, or as a private estate, are in principle monarchical. This is, in reality, the radical distinction between republicanism and monarchy,

and between civilization and barbarism, and it is so the terms should be understood.²²

Furthermore, in rejecting the patriarchal theory as an attempt to account for the moral rightness of government, Brownson has eliminated entirely the possibility of accounting for authority on a purely human basis. For he has shown already that the authority of government is not something which may be instituted by the people, either as individuals or as a political community. If the people as individuals institute its authority, government can be nothing more than the creature of the individual. Having been created by individuals it cannot exercise authority over them, for the creature has no authority over his creator.

On the other hand, government cannot be derived from the people as a community. For if the political community were the source of its own authority, it would be The Sovereign. This is despotism, socialism, caesaristic or humanitarian democracy.

Thus the position of Brownson in regard to the origin of authority is more clearly defined. Having demonstrated the impossibility of legitimating government on a purely human basis, Brownson maintains that it is necessary to reject, plainly and unequivocally, the authority of civil government, or else admit that its authority is derived from God. Thus anyone conceding the existence and the legitimacy of civil government can deny the existence of God only at the expense of logical consistency. On this point Brownson himself was consistent for he says that: "When I believed in no God I believed in no government . . . When I renounced my atheism I derived all power from God, the source of all law and of all justice."²³

It is evident, therefore, that Brownson must hold that political authority is derived from God. Having shown already that it must inhere in a republic, Brownson's theory must include the view that the ruler derives authority from

God through the people. In adopting this position Brownson believes he is accepting the traditional view of Catholic theologians, including both Suarez and St. Thomas. He believes, however, that his own formulation of the theory is more accurate because it is more complete, for his own theory includes the explanation that the people derive authority through the natural law. Consequently he amends the theory to read: "The right of government to govern, or political authority, is derived by the collective people or society, from God through the law of nature. Rulers hold from God through the people or nation, and the people or nation hold from God through the natural law."[24]

Now it is in the light of this theory that Brownson endeavors to solve the fundamental problem of political philosophy, the reconciliation of public authority and individual liberty, thus avoiding both anarchy and despotism. In order to understand what is involved in his theory it is necessary to recall briefly that the natural law is law in the strict and proper sense of the term. It is imposed upon the rational creature by God. What is authorized under it is therefore obligatory, just as much so as that which is authorized by the revealed law. It is called natural because it is promulgated through the reason natural to man. It is distinct, but not separated from the supernatural. Thus the natural and the revealed law are distinct parts of one and the same divine law.

In view of the fact that the state derives authority through the natural law, which is an expression of God's will, individuals are obliged to obey its enactments. In obeying them the individual obeys God who has authorized it to legislate. Consequently civil allegiance is a moral virtue. Thus it is clear that the state has authority, and that its authority must be obeyed.[25]

Since the people hold authority from God, they hold it as they do all other things He has given them, as a trust, which is forfeited by its abuse. Since the authority vested in the people is not their own, they cannot do with it whatever they please. Therefore any enactments contrary to God's law, under which the people are authorized as legislators, are *ipso facto* null and void.[26] Furthermore, since the ruler holds authority from God through the people he is accountable to the people as well as to God for the use made of his authority.

On this basis the freedom — not the license — of the individual is secured. For freedom, it has been noted, consists not in being free from law, but in obedience to God's commands. The individual is free to do that which is right, and he has the right to do that which is not forbidden. In disobeying God's law the individual is neither right nor free. Such action is license, not liberty.

The state, being authorized by God, has the right to legislate. Having the right to legislate it cannot be right for the individual to resist any enactments not contrary to the law of God. If laws are contrary to God's law, they are not authorized by Him. Therefore they are not obligatory. Consequently the individual is free, and has the right to resist them, for the individual is always free to obey God.

In this theory authority and liberty are therefore united harmoniously. Individual rights are secured without resorting to extreme individualism or anarchy. The authority of the state is secured without asserting openly or by implication, socialism or despotism.

While the theoretical solution of the problem of authority and liberty is thus solved rather simply — inasmuch as God's will, which is never in contradiction with itself, is the source of both authority and liberty — its practical application is somewhat more difficult. For it is obvious that there may be, and frequently is, a conflict between the liberty of the individual and public authority. Therefore it is necessary to indicate briefly the basis on which the practical problem of authority and liberty may be solved.

It has already been noted that Brownson maintains that the problem may be solved only by the practical recognition of the supremacy of God and His law. If His law is not supreme, and recognized as such, then there is no moral law, no moral right or wrong. Being unable to demand obedience on moral grounds, the state has nothing to appeal to except its might. The individual, being unable to protect his freedom on moral grounds, must resort likewise to might. In other words, the failure to recognize God's law emancipates both the individual and the state from all moral obligation. Consequently it is inevitable that both will appeal or resort to might. Thus it is likewise inevitable that: "Today it (society) is torn by a revolution in favor of socialism; to-morrow it will be torn by another in favor of individualism, and without affecting any real progress by either revolution."[27] Thus the problem of authority and liberty cannot be solved without the practical recognition of God's supremacy.

Furthermore, the mere recognition of God's law, and the appeal to it by both the individual and the state, is not sufficient to settle practically the controversy between authority and liberty. It may be assumed that God's law is the criterion of right and wrong for both the individual and the state, thus defining the limits of the state's authority and the rights of the individual. Yet who is to define God's law if a practical conflict arises? If the political philosopher will concede nothing more than God's law, individuals, and the state, he is no closer to a solution of his problem than if he denied God's law and God entirely.[28] If the authority to define the limitation of the state's power is lodged in the individual he would be in a position to justify any sort of disobedience by appealing to his interpretation of God's law particularly when enactments seemed inconvenient to him. Similarly if the state is the judge of its own cause, it may justify every act of tyranny. Socialism, for example, professes to be Christian, and it is in the name of Christianity that it contends for equality and the subsequent abolition of property.

In this way Brownson endeavors to show that if political authority is based either upon a total rejection of God's law, or upon God's law privately interpreted, it is not based upon truth. Its foundation is false. There is not the remotest possibility of solving the problem of authority and liberty since the truth, in the light of which it must be solved, is lacking. Since a solution is impossible it is necessary to assert principles which, if adopted, lead either to anarchy or absolutism, revolution or passive obedience.

In order to solve the problem of authority and liberty it is consequently necessary to recognize the truth that God is not only supreme lawgiver, but also that He has constituted a church capable of determining infallibly what He has commanded. This is the truth. It is only by building upon it that individuals and society can progress. This is the message Brownson endeavored to convey to his public. The following is typical of his attitude:

> Since the government derives its authority from God, and is amenable to his law, evidently it can be tried only under that law, and before a court which has authority to declare it, and to pronounce judgment accordingly.
>
> But what shall be done in case there be no such court of competent jurisdiction? We reject the supposition. Almighty God could never give a law without instituting a court to declare it, and to judge its infractions. We, as Catholics, know what and where that court is, and therefore cannot be embarrassed by the question. If there are nations who have no such court, or who refuse to recognize the one Almighty God has established, that is their affair, not ours, and they, not we, are responsible for the embarrassments

to which they are subjected. They, undoubtedly, are obliged either to assert passive obedience and non-resistance, or to deny the legitimacy of any government by asserting the right of revolution; that is, they have no alternative but anarchy or despotism, as their history proves. But this is not our fault. We are not aware that we are obliged to exclude God and his church from our politics in order to accommodate ourselves to those who blaspheme the one and revile the other. We are not aware that we are obliged to renounce our reason, and reject the lessons of experience, because if we admit them, they prove that Almighty God has made his church essential to the maintenance of civil authority on the one hand, and of civil liberty on the other, — because they prove that the state can succeed no better than the individual without religion.[29]

This position of Brownson follows as a consequence of his view that the natural and the supernatural order, the natural and the revealed law, are distinct parts of one whole. Forming a unit, the natural and the supernatural are not separated; both are parts of God's plan. It is therefore false to conceive of them as separated and unrelated. A theory of political authority based upon the supposition that the state is or can be separated from spiritual authority is based upon a falsehood. It must fail.

While it is false to conceive of the state as entirely separated from the church, it is equally false not to distinguish between them. For the channel through which the state derives its authority from God is the natural law, which is distinct from the revealed law. The state does not therefore derive its authority through the church or the ecclesiastical authorities.[30] It follows that since the state and church derive their authority from God through distinct channels and exist in distinct orders, neither can absorb the other. They are and must remain distinct as external governing bodies.[31]

In order to complete and to summarize Brownson's views on the nature and origin of authority, it is necessary to note that he has criticized and rejected in part, seven contrary theories before formulating his own.[32] His criticism of each theory is voluminous and somewhat repetitious, and not at all essential to the comprehension of his own theory. The brief statement of each theory which follows indicates that his reasons for rejecting it have already been incorporated in the chapter.

I. The patriarchal theory is rejected as an attempt to account for the moral rightness of government. It is essentially despotic because authority is considered a private right. In order to transform authority into a public trust territory must be introduced as a constituent element of political authority. Thus the state and its authority is a *res publica*.[33]

II. The social contract theory must be rejected because government is the creature of the individual. As such it can have no authority over the individual, who is its creator.[34]

III. The democratic theory must be rejected because it goes to the opposite extreme. The practical adoption of the theory would result in despotism or absolutism. It has an element of truth inasmuch as it invests authority in the people collectively or the community.[35]

IV. There is a theory which states that government is a development of nature. If the theory holds that it is nature in the sense of a spontaneous development independently of God's will the theory is wrong. It is the natural law, which is an expression of God's will that accounts for the moral rightness of government.[36]

V. The next theory which is criticised maintains that rulers hold their authority directly from God and not through the nation. This is the doctrine of the divine right of kings. The sole redeeming feature in the theory is that it derives power from God. But ". . . it consecrates tyranny, and makes God the accomplice of the tyrant."[37] In other words, it asserts the unlimited power of the ruler which is despotism.

VI. Another theory of the origin of authority states that political authority comes from God through the pope. This theory must be rejected because the state derives its authority from the natural law which is distinct from the revealed law.[38]

VII. The traditional doctrine of Catholic theologians asserts that rulers derive authority from God through the people. This view is sound and must be adopted without reservation. However, it does not state explicitly that authority comes from God through the natural law.[39]

VIII. "The right of Government to govern, or political authority, is derived by the collective people or society, from God through the law of nature. Rulers hold from God through the people or nation, and the people or nation hold from God through the natural law."[40] When the implications of this theory are unfolded, it is discovered that it contains all of the truths and none of the errors of the previous theories. It asserts, neither openly or by implication, anarchy or despotism. Thus it solves the fundamental problem of political philosophy, the reconciliation of authority and liberty.

It solves the problem not only theoretically, but also practically. In viewing the natural and revealed laws as distinct but not separate parts of one divine law, the state can never be separated from the church, which is the representative of God on earth capable of declaring infallibly God's law. On any other basis, such as a denial of either God's law or His church it is impossible to reconcile public authority with individual liberty.

Having thus disposed of the question of the nature and origin of authority, Brownson turns his attention to the state in which that authority resides. He has already limited the state in terms of its function, for the extremes to be avoided in its activity are anarchy and absolutism. In doing so Brownson obviously places a limitation upon the nature which he may attribute to it, for the nature of anything is the source of its activity. He cannot on the one hand attribute to it a nature whose parts are held together so loosely that it is in constant danger of disintegration, for he has affirmed the necessity of its continued existence as an organization having the authority to govern. Otherwise there would be anarchy. Again, he cannot give it a nature whose parts form a unit so completely that the existence of the individual, as a being with rights of his own, is endangered. Thus the boundaries within which Brownson must pursue his discussion of the state are already clearly defined.

5

THE NATURE OF THE STATE

BROWNSON'S exposition of the nature of the state rests upon various philosophical foundations.[1] Unfortunately he has no formal treatise on the state in which he presents in an orderly fashion his view of the constituent elements of the state. It is consequently necessary to impose an order upon Brownson's view of the state, and perhaps correct certain terminological inaccuracies.[2] He says that: "Sovereignty, under God inheres in the organic people, or in the people as the republic; and every organic people fixed to the soil, and politically independent of every other people, is a sovereign people, and, in the modern sense, an independent sovereign nation."[3]

Brownson's conception of the state as an organism is derived from his interpretation of the Platonic theory of ideas. According to Plato's theory, humanity is an idea. It exists in the divine mind as a simple, indivisible, generative principle. Its activity results in the production of individual men and women. It is to the individual ". . . what the principle of vitality or vital force is to the human body."[4]

Now according to Brownson the vital force of the individual is its unifying principle; it makes the members of his body parts of one whole.[5] For example, the eyes and ears of the human body are related as members of one body because they derive their vitality from the simple, vital force which pervades the entire body and makes it one.

Similarly, individuals derive their vitality from one and the same vital force. This is humanity. Since it is one and simple, it pervades all individuals equally. Therefore it unites individuals as members of an organism; it makes them parts of one body. Thus Brownson says that society is not merely an association of individuals, but a "Living Organism."[6]

The development of this analogy gives us a true picture of the nature of society. Since it is an organism, it follows that society has different members. It follows also that each individual, considered as a member of the organism, has a specific function, just as the function of the eye is to see and the ear to hear.[7] However, Brownson points out, "What is essential to the life and growth of the whole is, that each member be preserved in his sound and healthy state so as to be able to perform without obstruction, his special function."[8]

This means, therefore, that men's welfare and that of society are intimately interwoven. Society is in a sense the completion of man because it fills up a need that is rooted in his nature. The reason for this is that man's nature is at once individual and social. The humanity which constitutes him an individual is the same humanity that unites him to others as a member of an organism. Consequently he cannot exist without deriving life from the organism of which he is a member, any more than the eye could exist apart from the body.[9]

Thus far Brownson has said nothing explicitly about the state. He has given us a conception of individuals who cannot exist apart from society. Since the individual cannot exist apart from it, his relationship to society is that of a member who cannot exist if it is cut off from the body to which it belongs. His procedure is clear, however, inasmuch as he has already established the fact that government is necessary to society. He has shown that the family, which is the smallest society from the numerical standpoint, cannot exist without government because it would fail for lack of unity.[10] Consequently government is introduced as the factor which renders effective man's existence as a member of an organism.[11]

In other words, government is necessary to society just as society is necessary to man. Being essential and indispensable to society, which in turn is necessary for man, government must exist as the condition upon which man expresses or actualizes his nature. Thus Brownson says, "Extinguish government and you extinguish society; extinguish society and you extinguish man."[12]

Now government exists in both the family and in the republic or a people fixed to a territory. Parental authority, however, is confined within the narrow limits of an immediate family. Being legitimate only within a family, it ceases to be legitimate with the natural growth and expansion of the family. Consequently the government of the parent or the patriarch must be replaced or transformed into that of the state in order to be legitimate. The family grows and expands naturally into a larger society, but the father can have no natural right to govern a society larger than his immediate family. Consequently authority in such a society must be based upon something other than the conjugal relationship. It has been indicated already that the basis of this authority must be something common, a *res publica,* or a territory commonly held.[13]

Being an organism, the state is required to secure the good of the individuals constituting it as the condition of securing its own welfare. It has been noted previously that the welfare of the whole depends upon the welfare of its parts. Now the individual is at once an individual and a member of society.[14] Therefore in order to secure the good of the individual the state must permit him to fulfill his function both as an individual and as a member of society.

Since government is necessary for society, which in turn is necessary for man, there is no intimation in Brownson of the view that government is a necessary evil, or that it is rendered necessary by man's fall. Its function is positive rather than negative. It is the condition upon which man may develop and perfect his natural capacities. Consequently it is a good for man, second only to religion. In Brownson's words:

> It is needed to render effective the solidarity of the individuals of a nation, and to render them an organism, not a mere organization—to combine men in one living body, and to strengthen all with the strength of each, and each with the strength of all — to develop, strengthen, and sustain individual liberty, and to utilize and direct it to the promotion of the commonwealth — to be a social providence, imitating in its order and degree the action of the divine providence itself, and, while it provides for the common good of all, to protect each, the lowest and meanest, with the whole force and majesty of society. It is the minister of wrath to wrong-doers, indeed, but its nature is beneficent, and its action defines and protects the right of property, creates and maintains a medium in which religion can exert her supernatural energy, promotes learning, fosters science and art, advances civilization, and contributes as a powerful means to the fulfillment by man of the divine purpose of his existence. Next after religion, it is man's greatest good; and even religion without it can do only a small portion of her work. They wrong it who call it a necessary evil; it is a great good, and, instead of being distrusted, hated, or resisted, except in its abuses, it should be loved, respected, obeyed, and, if need be, defended at the cost of all earthly goods, and even of life itself.[15]

Thus far Brownson has said that the state fulfills a need existing in man's nature and that it is consequently a good.

He has said also that its authority inheres in the people as a whole and is consequently the attribute of the whole organism rather than of any individual.

At this time, however, Brownson introduces doctrines which are not precisely ordinary, at least not with respect to the manner in which he expressed them. The first of these doctrines is introduced to explain why or how people come to be organized into particular states. That is, he endeavors to indicate the basic factors which unify a people and give it a distinctive existence as a people.

Adopting his usual procedure, Brownson begins by criticising contrary theories before presenting his own view. He begins by denying that a written document, ordinarily referred to as a constitution, is the basic or fundamental factor which organizes people into a state. A written constitution, being the act of community of a people, obviously presupposes the existence of individuals already organized in some way. Since it presupposes an organized people, a constitution cannot be the sole organizing factor of a people.[16] In other words, on the supposition that a written constitution is the fundamental factor which unifies a people or gives being to them, it would be possible to conceive of a state as a purely artificial production. The nation would be similar to ". . . a temperance society or debating club, a simple voluntary association which men are free to join or not as they please."[17] Thus Brownson rejects entirely the view that states come into existence or can be formed suddenly, created *de novo*, by the formulation of a written constitution.

In opposition to the contract theory of Rousseau, Brownson says that states come into existence by a process of growth or development, rather than a production. That which constitutes or unifies a people is its own internal organization, represented in the habits, the manners, the customs, the living traditions which grow and develop as a people grow and develop. It is this internal organization which gives the state its vitality, ". . . that which controls or governs its action, and determines its destiny."[18]

Now the habits, manners, traditions, customs of a people that come into existence by a process of growth or development represent, for Brownson, an internal unifying factor which precedes, and is more fundamental, than its written constitution. He speaks of the sum of these factors in terms of an organic, or unwritten, constitution,[19] or in terms of its unwritten or living law.[20]

The point that Brownson endeavors to convey, in terms which appear somewhat confusing, is the fact that an individual government must be adapted to, and be an expression of, the fundamental and distinctive habits and traditions of a people. It cannot be created artificially and imposed from without. "It must be born and developed with the nation . . . Constitutions of states are not things that can be made to order, and imposed by authority, regardless of the habits, manners, customs, and traditions of the people who are to live under them."[21]

This means that if, for example, a monarch is included in the fundamental, internal organization of a people, it is the sheerest folly to remove the monarch and attempt to impose another form which has no basis in the traditions of a people.

> The French people adopted constitution after constitution of the most approved pattern, and amid bonfires, beating of drums, sound of trumpets, roar of musketry, and thunder of artillery, swore, no doubt, sincerely as well as enthusiastically, to observe them, but all to no effect; for they had no authority for the nation, no hold on its affection, and formed no element of its life.[22]

Brownson believes, therefore, that the fundamental and primary organization of a people determines the particular form of government which is most suitable for that people.

He could never bring himself to consider seriously the question as to whether or not one form of government is inherently better than another.[23] "The constitution of government must grow out of the constitution of the state, and accord with the genius, the character, the habits, customs, and wants of the people, or it will not work well, or tend to secure the legitimate ends of government."[24]

In other words, Brownson holds that a people develops a unity or organization which is distinctively its own. Anything rooted in that organization as an integral element, cannot be uprooted without destroying the people. Consequently a government imposed from without tends to eliminate or destroy a radical element of that organization. Such a government seldom, if ever, has a hold on the people and is consequently seldom a good government. It must be maintained by force because it is not the expression of a living organism.

Brownson also attempts to answer the question as to why or how people become organized on a territorial basis and thus begin to exist as states, and why some survive and others are extinguished. His answer, whether philosophical or not, is that the providence of God is the only ultimate explanation. God in His providence has permitted states to be extinguished, and some of them by violence. Why He has done so ". . . is no question for the statesman; it is the secret of Providence. Failure in this world is not always a proof of wrong; nor success, of right. The good is sometimes overborne, and the bad sometimes triumphs; but it is consoling, and even just, to believe that the good oftener triumphs over the bad."[25]

Likewise, God in His providence is ultimately responsible for the existence of a particular people, state, or nation. Consequently Brownson also refers to the organic or unwritten constitution which gives being to a state as its providential constitution.[26] In order to discover what he means by it, it is necessary to discover what he means by providence and thus determine the respective roles of providence and human agency in the formation of the state.

Providence, for Brownson, means the action by which God sustains, cooperates with, and directs His creatures: "Providence is as necessary as creation, or rather, providence is only continuous creation, the creative act not suspended or discontinued, or not passing over from the creature and returning to God."[27] He distinguishes between God's providence and God's natural law: "The law of nature is not the order or rule of the divine action in nature which is rightfully called providence . . ."[28]

The necessity for the divine action in nature called providence is to be found in the nature of the creature. He is a second cause, a substantial existence, but nevertheless dependent; consequently God must concur, cooperate with, and direct every action of every creature. Having given man a nature which is free, God must direct him, but he ". . . must leave his freedom intact . . . How this can be done, we do not undertake to say."[29]

Applying this doctrine to the state, Brownson says that men cannot produce a state *de novo*. A germinal organization must be given them to start with. This germinal organization which men cannot produce is present in families, in families united into tribes. It develops in the migrations of families and in colonies through wars, conquests, rebellions, amalgamation of conquered and conqueror. In a word, the development of a nation presupposes a germinal organization which may be developed.[30]

Now Brownson maintains that it is by reason of circumstances such as those mentioned that nations begin to exist. These circumstances are providential in his estimation, but not therefore fatalistic.[31] The germ which is given to a people by reason of these events is not, properly speaking, made; it is rather a generation. Granted such a germinal organization, men may develop it. They may develop distinctive habits, customs, and instinctive unity as a people, but they cannot by their own voluntary efforts bring into existence or produce the germinal organization they have to begin with. This is the work of providence.[32]

As an indication of what Brownson means by the providential constitution with respect to human liberty in its formation the following brief passages are cited:

> ... constitutions are generated, or developed, not created *de novo,* or made all at once. But nothing is more sure than that a nation can alter its constitution by its own deliberate and voluntary action, and many nations have done so, and sometimes for the better as well as the worse.[33]
>
> Providence is always present in the affairs of nations, but not to work miracles to counteract the natural effects of the ignorance, ineptness, short-sightedness, narrow views, public stupidity, and imbecility of rulers, because they are irreproachable and saintly in their private characters and relations.[34]

The doctrine presented thus far means that Brownson has established the fact that the state is an organic people fixed to a territory. On the basis of his analysis of man's nature, he has shown that man is related to society as an organ is related to the body from which it draws life. Society requires authority, which in turn exists only in people related territorially. The possession of both territory and living traditions are unifying factors of the state which precede the adoption of its written constitution. Thus the state is an organic people fixed to a territory.

The consequences which Brownson draws from this position are, if nothing else, at least somewhat startling. Brownson argues that if political authority is an attribute of the people as a whole, it cannot be prior to, but must be consequent upon, the existence of an organism. Unfortunately, Brownson states the conclusion derived from this position rather abruptly and without sufficient warning, for he says in no uncertain terms that "A nation *de facto* is a nation *de jure,* and when we have ascertained the fact, we have ascertained the right. There is no right in the case separate from the fact."[35]

It is rather unfortunate that Brownson's arguments are stated somewhat vehemently and abruptly on any side of a question because it is rather easy to select certain passages, such as that above, and prove that Brownson was an advocate of the doctrine that might makes right. It is also easy to select passages from Brownson to prove that he was an anarchist. Brownson himself notes this, and rather frequently, when he says that "We are not infrequently accused of being one-sided, narrow-minded, and disposed always to push the principles we may have happened to adopt to extreme. Nothing is more untrue."[36] And again:

> . . . if we oppose false liberty, or license presented under the name of liberty, we are charged with being enemies of true freedom; if we assert authority, however legitimate or necessary, then we are despots or advocates of despotism. The press opens its cry against us, and the age votes us mediaeval dreamers, behind the times, relics of the past, with our eyes on the backside of our heads, and the truth is drowned in the floods of indignation or ridicule poured out against us.[37]

Since Brownson was notoriously imprudent and extreme it is necessary to present his doctrine more prudently, without thereby presenting it less accurately, or with a view to suppressing his doctrine for the purpose of vindicating it.

In view of the fact that Brownson maintains that political sovereignty vests in the political community, or the state, or the people as an organism, he distinguishes sharply between the state and the government commissioned under it: "The government, as distinguished from the state or nation, has only a delegated authority, governs only by a commission from the nation. The revocation of the commission vacates its title and extinguishes its right."[38]

In other words, the people, being sovereign, may commission this government or that; they may entrust authority to a king or an aristocracy, or to a combination. The distinction between the sovereign people and the government is that between the sovereign and his agent.[39] This means that no ruler, whether he be king or emperor, holds his authority as he does a piece of property.[40] The people may, for a good and sufficient reason, dismiss their agent, whether he be called king or emperor, without depriving him of any indefeasible right, as they would do if they deprived him of property. "The right of a nation to change its form of government, and its magistrates or representatives, by whatever name called, is incontestable."[41]

This according to Brownson, is nothing more than the logical application of the doctrine that sovereignty vests in the people, and that rulers are consequently justifiable by the people as well as by God for the use made of authority.[42] Although sovereignty is delegated to rulers, sovereignty itself is in the people and persists in them. The powers delegated to government ". . . are still the powers of the sovereign delegating them, and may be modified, altered, or revoked, as the sovereign judges proper."[43]

Applying this doctrine still further, Brownson holds that an existing government may be destroyed entirely without thereby destroying the state or the sovereignty of the people. If the people survive the destruction of their government, ". . . the sovereign remains in the plentitude of his rights, as competent to restore government as he was originally to institute it."[44]

It may happen further that a particular ruler or a particular government may be overthrown, not by the people acting as sovereign, but by a mob. Subsequently a new ruler may acquire his position by an act that is manifestly unjust.[45] In such a case Brownson contends that the people still maintain the right to legalize, or to legitimate, the title of the new ruler. The fact that the people will to retain a ruler is in itself sufficient to give him legitimate authority. His right as a ruler is not derived from any right prior to the will of the people, for "He holds his power, as the emperor of the French professes to hold his, by the grace of God and the national will — the only title by which a king or emperor can legitimately hold power."[46]

It is clear therefore, that Brownson's doctrine does not mean that a *government de facto* is a *government de jure*. One who acquires title by violence may be the ruler *de facto*, but he does not rule *de jure* unless the people he rules will to retain him as ruler. If he maintains power by mere force he is a tyrant, a usurper without authority.

According to Brownson a clear cut case of a government that is *de facto* imposed upon the people without being *de jure* is England's dominion in India.[47] Its dominion is *de facto*, but it is without right and consequently tyrannical. It is government without legitimate authority to govern and therefore barbaric and despotic in principle. England may succeed in maintaining it, according to Brownson, but if it does it will ". . . wreak a vengeance on the unhappy Hindoos that will establish her character for cruelty and barbarity down to the end of the world."[48]

With the distinction between state and government clearly in mind it is impossible to maintain that Brownson holds that every government able to preserve itself by force is a *de jure* government. It is consequently necessary to examine his assertion that every nation *de facto* is a nation *de jure* on the basis of this distinction.

In asserting that a nation *de facto* is a nation *de jure*, Brownson was endeavoring to discover the basis on which the state derives authority from God. He rejects the view that a state, in order to be legitimate, must have come into existence rightfully. His reason for rejecting this view is made on the ground that it would be impossible to justify, or to assert the rightful existence of, a single civilized state:

> A hundred or more lost nationalities went to form the Roman empire, and who can tell us how many layers of crushed nationalities, superimposed one upon another, serve for the foundation of the present French, English, Russian, Austrian, or Spanish nationality. What other title to independence and sovereignty, than the fact, can you plead in behalf of any European nation? Every one has absorbed and extinguished — no one can say how many — nationalities, that once had as good a right to be as it has, or can have.[49]

This argument is typical of Brownson. He says that if a nation must be founded rightfully in order to be just, accept the principle and apply it regardless of the consequences: ". . . I have never in my life been able to persuade myself that a principle, really sound and true, will not bear pushing to its last logical consequences."[50] He continues that if a principle cannot be applied, it is proof that it is untrue and cannot be adopted. Obviously, as has been indicated, he maintains that the principle that a nation must be founded rightfully in order to possess legitimate authority cannot be a criterion for determining its legitimacy.

Rejecting this view as untenable, Brownson accepts the consequences of the doctrine that authority inheres in the state as an attribute of the whole organism. As such it is necessarily consequent upon, and not prior to, the existence of the organism. Therefore it begins with the existence of the organism and is extinguished with its death: "There is no right behind the fact needed to legalize the fact, or to put the nation that is in fact a nation in possession of full national rights."[51]

The doctrine that a nation, not a government, *de facto* is a nation *de jure,* taken in connection with his view on the origin of authority, serves to unify and to render more definite Brownson's view of the state. He has maintained that authority comes from God through the natural law. It inheres in the state as an organism for the good of the whole. The state is constituted or given existence by the possession of a territory and by a distinctive internal organization of its own. Thus the authority of the state inheres in the state itself. A written enactment is consequently not constitutive: it is the product of, or is written by, a people already existing as a people.

Since Brownson maintains that a nation *de facto* is a nation *de jure,* he maintains that the existence of a nation is simply a question of historical fact. The functions of a sovereign are easily discernible, as easily as any other historical fact. Briefly, the distinctive characteristic of sovereignty is the exercise of complete authority, which is the management of both internal and external, foreign and domestic affairs.[52]

Since Brownson maintains that the existence of a nation is a simple question of historical fact, he is merely applying his doctrine that its authority remains and persists in the organic constitution. With respect to India, for example, the historical fact is evident. The internal organizations have not been broken. Consequently there remains the right to resist invaders, who are of necessity tyrants. On the other hand, a people whose distinctive organizations have been broken, who have been absorbed, assimilated, conquered, are no longer *de facto* a people. As scattered remnants they have no longer the right to institute and exercise complete political authority.[53]

His thought is indicated clearly with respect to colonies existing under the jurisdiction of their mother country. Such colonies are not sovereign *de facto*. They may exercise some of the functions of a sovereign such as the control of domestic affairs. Such authority is legitimate; it is authorized through the political sovereign. If the authority of the mother country over its colonies is such that it is tyrannical, oppressive, too great to be endured, it may be resisted even by force. This may be, but seldom is the case.

Yet a people dependent upon legitimate political authority may *never* revolt against it merely to secure complete political authority or sovereignty for themselves. To maintain the contrary that is, that individuals, groups, colonies, are inherently sovereign and have the *right* to be sovereign, is to babble the nonsense of Rousseau. It would, if adopted in principle, put an end to all legitimacy:

> Myself and two others might otherwise unite, and declare ourselves a sovereign state, and secede from the city, the state, and the Union, and scornfully refuse to recognize your magistrates, your laws, your police, your conscription, and your tax-bills. This would be democracy run mad, and too absurd to be asserted even by the Evening Post or the New York Tribune.[54]

Brownson has maintained that a people always begin existence with a germinal organization which is given to it. This organization grows with the people; it develops with them. It becomes a part of the living, breathing people themselves. This organization is represented in the living habits, traditions and institutions of a people. This living, growing organization is a unifying factor which is more important than written enactments.

If such a people are in possession of a territory, and they are politically dependent, they are not sovereign. They hold authority dependently upon the sovereign who has authorized their existence. Such authority is legitimate; it is right. Consequently it cannot be right to revolt against it merely in order to obtain complete authority.

If it were accepted as a matter of principle that such a people could revolt for the purpose of securing complete authority for themselves, one would accept, consciously so or not, the principle that people are in themselves sovereign.

Being sovereign they have a right to unite voluntarily, to ordain government, to revolt in order to secure complete authority. Thus Brownson maintains that if there could be a *right* to complete authority prior to the fact, one would be in the absurd position of maintaining that it is right for a colony to resist the rightful enactments of the mother country.

On the other hand, if such a colony does revolt *de facto* it thereby severs the channel through which it derived legitimate authority. Since it has been cut off from the source of its authority, (1) it must be left without authority, or (2) its authority must be derived from some other source. (3) The source can be none other than that indicated by Brownson in the exposition of his own doctrine.

(1) Authority exists only in the state. The colony is a transplanted dependent group, deriving authority legitimately through the mother country. If by a wrongful act they sever that channel, it is impossible for them to convene as isolated individuals and re-institute, by a convention, a legitimate government. They cannot, in other words, make their government a rightful government by surrendering rights, agreeing to be governed, or consenting voluntarily; in a word, their government cannot be legitimated in terms of Rousseau's social contract. Thus, if the channel through which legitimate authority is derived is severed, and if the state must come into existence rightfully, there is no possible way for Brownson to introduce legitimacy into any government of Europe, and more importantly, into the government of the United States.

(2) Having severed the channel from which they derived authority, Brownson endeavors to discover a new channel through which authority may be derived. It cannot come from God through separate individuals, because individuals, again are equal. God has given to man no dominion over man. Further, authority obviously could not be derived through the written enactments existing in virtue of the

authority of Britain. With the termination of the authority through which the written documents were authorized, they were no longer law. Thus individuals as such and any previously existing written documents are eliminated of necessity for Brownson as a means whereby, or as channels through which, any new enactments might be legitimated.

(3) Brownson solves the problem, of course, on the basis of his conception of authority as derived from God through the law of nature. It is given to the nation when it exists as such. It inheres in the people as an organism, fixed to a territory. The people are constituted a people by the presence of living institutions and traditions which are prior to, and able to survive the destruction of, written documents. Thus with the termination of the war, authority, under God, inhered — not certainly in Americans as individuals — somewhere in the living organizations which persisted despite the termination of the authority of their written documents.

6

THE UNION OF STATES

IT HAS been noted in a previous chapter that after the election of 1840, Brownson's theory and the reality confronting him refused to harmonize. The infallible people had betrayed their birthright for a barrel of cider. Being thus rudely awakened, Brownson was driven to an examination of the principles upon which he had based his views.

A somewhat similar situation confronted Brownson during the period preceding the civil war. His comments upon practical affairs were based upon the principle that the Union is a confederacy of independent states or nations. He notes later that "This view is simple, and is easily taken in, and we confess we held and defended it down almost to the breaking out of the rebellion."[1] As secession threatened he found himself on the side of the Union. Here again was a situation in which his theory and the concrete reality confronting him refused to harmonize.

His procedure was similar to that followed in 1840. First of all he tested his theory for consistency. He had reasoned that if the states were in the beginning sovereign and independent, then the relationship between state and union is that of the sovereign to his agent. He had supplied the fact that they were sovereign when they began their existence as states. The conclusion is inescapable. Finding no flaws in his reasoning, or that of Calhoun to which it is similar, his only alternative was to examine the fact which he had taken in and assumed to be true.

Now the terms in which Brownson's investigation must be conducted have been indicated in the concluding remarks of the preceding chapter. He has maintained that the formation of a nation or a people with a distinctive internal organization or constitution of its own is a process of growth and development rather than a production. On the basis of his theory, a people are constituted by the development of distinctive habits, customs, living traditions and institutions — not by the production of a written document. Consequently he is obliged to investigate the formative period of the nation, for this period reveals its radical and distinctive elements.

In addition to this view Brownson has maintained that the government of the people must be rooted in these elements. It must retain them. If it does so it is invigorated by the life blood of the nation itself. If it tends to eliminate anything radical, it can be maintained only by physical force. Consequently the conclusion of the investigation reveals Brownson's conception of the organic constitution to which the existing government must conform in order to maintain the American Republic.

The immediate results of Brownson's investigation, to the surprise of no one, reveals the fact that he had been wrong in assuming without a thorough investigation that the states were originally sovereign. In terms of vindicating either North or South, his arguments leading to that conclusion are unimportant. They are, however, indispensable for a comprehension of Brownson's interpretation of an existing reality. It is for this reason that it is necessary to begin with his presentation of the argument for an original nation.

Since it is Brownson's avowed purpose to discuss the organic constitution, which cannot be embodied completely in written documents, his case for union cannot rest entirely upon an interpretation of a document such as the Articles of Confederation. He concedes that those who formulated these documents looked upon the union as a compact between sovereign states. But he also remarks that these men, for the most part, looked upon the state itself as a compact entered into by sovereign individuals, as is evident in the statement that government derives its legitimacy from the consent of the governed.[2]

Brownson argues that the mere fact that some individuals of the period viewed society as though it were a temperance society does not mean that the society called the state is really that kind of organization. It is not a simple, voluntary association despite the fact that these men thought so. Likewise, the fact that some men thought they were forming a simple contract between sovereign states does not imply that their thoughts on the matter were in conformity with reality. The real intention of those in authority has something to do with the matter, but it is not the court of last resort beyond which there is no appeal. Consequently the crux of the issue is the reality itself rather than previous interpretations of it.[3]

Thus there are in a sense two courts in which the case for an original union of states may be tried. One of these is obviously the written documents, such as the Declaration of Independence, the Articles of Confederation and the Constitution as amended by the convention of 1787. However, to the extent that these documents embody the philosophy of those who framed them, such as the view that government derives its just powers from the consent of the governed, they include opinions or interpretations of an existing situation. Since Brownson has questioned the philosophical basis of such opinion, he is led to question the opinions and interpretations of the founding fathers. Thus their opinions represent a court in which the case may be tried, but it does not represent the supreme court from whose decision there is no appeal. The other court, the supreme court, is the existing situation itself independently of previous interpretations.

Brownson states the case in commenting upon the philosophical judgment of the founding fathers.

> Men may have a good understanding of facts and yet fail utterly, and become grossly absurd, when they attempt to construct theories for their explanation. The question for us is, not what theories our fathers held with regard to the seat of the sovereign power, but where it was actually lodged as a matter of fact, for the fact overrides all theories on the subject.[4]

Brownson's view is of course based upon the doctrine presented in the preceding chapter, that a nation *de facto* is a nation *de jure*. A nation derives authority from God by the fact that it exists and maintains itself. If an organized people institute civil government and exercise within and without the functions consequent upon a nation, they are by that very fact invested with authority. The rightfulness, or lack of it, by which a nation comes into existence is not the criterion for determining whether or not it has authority. Nations like individuals have rights as soon as they exist. Attempts to determine an antecedent rightfulness in either case are grossly absurd.

This means first of all that Brownson is not required to justify the revolution by which the colonies acquired a status as a nation. The United States has legitimate authority regardless of whether or not the revolution was justified.[5] It means secondly that since sovereignty is a fact and not a right prior to the fact, there is no *a priori* ground on which it is possible to determine whether sovereignty existed in the states or in the union.[6]

This means that Brownson must discount arguments designed to show an antecedent rightfulness of each state to sovereignty. There is no right prior to the fact of sovereignty. It means, too, that he must throw out of court arguments designed to show that each state thought it was sovereign and had the right to be sovereign. The men who thought this way also thought that society itself was composed of individuals who are sovereign in their own right. Accepting the theory that the state itself derives legitimate authority because sovereign individuals surrender rights to it, it was natural for them to speak of a union of states in terms of rights surrendered by sovereign states.

Brownson's basis for ascertaining an original union of states is thus clearly defined:

> The historical fact determines who is the sovereign, who are the sovereign people, where, in a sovereign nation, the sovereignty is lodged, and through what channels it is exercised; because the existence and constitution of the national sovereignty is an historical fact, anterior to all written constitutions and to all positive legislative enactments. What might have been, what is desirable, should have been, are political and ethical questions, — very interesting, very important, no doubt, but of no moment in determining what is.[7]

The facts which Brownson presents briefly are the following. The original unit of organization was the colony. Further,

> ... the colonies were mutually separate and independent political corporations, or, if you prefer, political communities before the Union existed, and, unless in the British people, did in no sense constitute one political community. We do not pretend, and do not recollect, that we ever have pretended, that, distinguished from their unity under the British crown and parliament, they were *always* one political people ... They were originally separate and mutually independent political communities.[8]

Another fact: The people acting through colonial organizations waged a war for independence. With the termination of the war, the sovereignty of Britain with reference to the colonies was terminated. The Crown was no longer the sovereign as a fact and consequently was not rightfully sovereign. But sovereignty did not lapse. It passed to those who won independence as a fact and as a matter of fact exercised it:

> Sovereignty never lapses, is never in abeyance, and the moment it ceases in one people it is renewed in another. The British sovereignty ceased in the colonies with independence, and the American took its place. Did the sovereignty, which before independence was in Great Britain, pass from Great Britain to the states severally, or to the states united? It might have passed to them severally, but did it? There is no question of law or antecedent right in the case, but a simple question of fact, and the fact is determined by determining who it was that assumed it, exercised it, and has continued to exercise it.[9]

Brownson maintains that the obvious fact of the matter is that people acting through colonial organizations waged the successful war for independence. It is further obvious that the colonial organizations did not merge to the extent that they lost their identity as distinct organizations; but it it equally obvious that they were not separated to the extent that they did not act jointly.

At this point it must be noted that Brownson nowhere attempts to explain why the colonies acted jointly. There is no intimation in his doctrine that the colonies united because of a mutual love for one another, or with the avowed intention of forming one nation. Nor is there an attempt made to discover why the people were distributed into colonies which acted jointly: "How they became so united and so divided is of no consequence in determining what was or is the real constitution of the American people."[10] Whatever reasons may be alleged to explain it, the fact remains that people distributed into colonial organizations acting jointly through these organizations waged a successful war.

Having maintained that sovereignty was wrested from Britain by the joint action of people existing in distinct political corporations, Brownson must endeavor to defend the thesis that it was exercised in the same way that it was secured. In his estimation a sovereign nation is one which maintains, within and without, the functions consequent upon every civilized nation.

Brownson is obliged to show first of all that with the termination of the war political authority remained in, and continued to be exercised by distinct political corporations. Secondly, he is obliged to show that these political corporations continued to act jointly. No one of these distinct communities exercised and continued to exercise *de facto* the functions consequent upon a civilized nation. Consequently they were never independent nations *de facto*, and therefore not *de jure*.

Brownson argues that after independence the states continued to exercise the functions formerly performed by them as colonies. There was therefore a continuity of function from colony to successfully rebelled colony or state. The people who rebelled through distinct organizations continued to act through distinct communities after the rebellion. Consequently it is certain that ". . . the political people of the United States have never existed as a consolidated mass, without organization or distribution into separate and mutually independent states, corporations, or political societies."[11]

It is equally certain that the individual state has never proved its ability to maintain civil government as a sovereign nation by fulfilling within and without the functions consequent upon such a nation.[12] The functions which it has failed to exercise as a fact are those which concern its relationship to foreign powers, such as the negotiation of treaties and the right to declare war.[13] Thus, ". . . bating a few irregularities not to be counted . . ." individual states have never existed and maintained themselves as individual nations fulfilling all of the functions consequent upon sovereignty.[14]

Brownson argues therefore that there is a continuity of function from Crown to individual-states-acting-jointly. In terms of a federal government, which at this point represents whatever alliance existed among the states, this means that the federal government performed the functions formerly reserved to the crown. Thus the function by reason of which the colony itself lacked complete political authority, which is the distinctive characteristic of a sovereign nation, is also lacking in the successfully rebelled colony or the state considered separately.[15]

Consistently with his theory of the organic constitution, which maintains that the formation of a state is a process of growth and development, Brownson does not and cannot maintain that a nation emerged from the struggle for independence with institutions fully formed and developed.[16] Consequently he does not and cannot maintain that there was a clearly defined line of demarcation between federal and state governments as early as 1776. For this reason irregularities existing during that period, or a confusion as to the precise function of each organization, are to be discounted, for these lines of demarcation are part of the development and formation of the nation. Thus he describes the period immediately following 1776 as a transitional period during which the nation was struggling for possession of the faculties whereby it could maintain its existence.

In its struggle to maintain itself, the people, acting through colonial organizations, adopted the Article of Confederation. The congress under it failed. It was acknowledged as a failure. The very fact of failure proves that the

Articles of Confederation were not in harmony with the needs and wants of the people. If they had met and had continued to meet the circumstances which confronted the people, there would have been no need to reject them. Their failure is consequently conclusive proof of the fact that the central government authorized under them was too weak.[17]

In terms of Brownson's organic constitution, the doctrine presented thus far means that the Union began with the distribution of people into distinct colonies under the Crown. While dependent upon the Crown the people began to act jointly through colonial organizations. The instinct or habit of acting jointly in this way was strengthened by the struggle for independence. Circumstances necessitated concerted action for success.

The instinct for concerted action which the people had developed, while present at the termination of the conflict, was not clearly recognized by the people themselves. Thus they formed a central government without taking into consideration the instinct for joint action which had already been formed. It was doomed to failure because it was not constructed in accordance with the needs and customs of the people who had to live under it. The fact that it was not in accord with the needs and wants of the people is proved by the fact that it failed.

Powers were more clearly defined under the institutions adopted subsequently. Individual states retained jurisdiction over particular interests, the general government over general affairs. Being incomplete, neither government performed the functions of a sovereign by itself. Consequently both governments are necessary for complete authority which is the distinctive characteristic of a nation. The fact that such an arrangement is in harmony with the basic structure and needs of the people is proved by its success.

Thus Brownson contends that it was a people acting jointly through colonial organizations who waged and won the war for independence. It was a people acting jointly through state organizations who proved themselves capable of performing within and without the functions consequent upon a civilized nation. Both particular communities and communities acting jointly are integral parts of the American Republic. Thus states are sovereign in union or joint action but not in separation.[18] Brownson is somewhat vague in regard to the point at which sovereignty lapsed in Britain and became a fact in the United States:

> Independence was declared in 1776, but it was not a fact till 1782, when the preliminary treaty acknowledging it was signed at Paris. Till then the United States were not an independent nation; they were only a people struggling to become an independent nation. Prior to that preliminary treaty, neither the Union nor the states severally were sovereign. The articles were agreed on in Congress in 1777, but they were not ratified by all the states till May, 1781, and in 1782 the movement was commenced in the legislature of New York for their amendment. Till the organization under the constitution ordained by the people of the United States in 1787, and which went into operation in 1789, the United States had in reality only a provisional government, and it was not till then that the national government was definitely organized, and the line of demarcation between the general government and the particular state governments was fixed.[19]

Before proceeding with Brownson's exposition of the union of states it is necessary to note that he attempts to gain additional support for his case by an interpretation of historical documents. Of his rather ingenious comments in this regard the following is typical. He says that the framers of the original Articles of Confederation called it "confederation, but only because they had not attained to full consciousness of themselves; and that they really meant union, not confederation, is evident from their adopting, as the official style of the nation or new power, *united,* not *confederate* states."[20]

A part of this statement is tenable inasmuch as the people who were required to meet rather pressing problems immediately after the war did not recognize clearly the extent of the joint action required to win the war and to maintain themselves. Thus the statement that the people had not attained to full consciousness of their institutions is tenable. Yet when Brownson adds that "They really meant union" and not confederation, he is clearly making a statement for which he can have no factual evidence. One would begin to suspect that Brownson had no insight into the minds of these men and consequently had no way of determining what they really meant or did not mean.

Brownson's position with regard to an interpretation of these documents is indicated in the following:

> There can be little doubt that the strongest nationalists in 1787, if they had been asked where was our political sovereignty prior to the adoption of the federal constitution, would have answered, in the states, or the people of the states, severally; and would have maintained, if pressed, that the national sovereignty they asserted was created by the surrender of a certain portion of the rights of the states to the general government. The possibility of such surrender nobody questioned, and nobody saw anything absurd in the assertion at once of the sovereignty of the Union and of the states severally ... Even in the preamble to the declaration of independence, by the congress of 1776, we find the assertion that "government derives its just powers from the consent of the governed." Holding this doctrine, the statesmen of 1787 could concede without difficulty that the states, or the people of the states severally, were sovereign prior to the adoption of the federal constitution, and yet

deny them to be sovereign afterwards . . . To concede the original sovereignty of the states severally, and then to deny the right of secession, is simply to outrage common sense.[21]

With this view of the philosophy prevailing at the time, Brownson says it is necessary and important to take such a factor into consideration in interpreting these historical documents. It is clear that the convention of 1787 recognized the fact that states had been acting jointly or in cooperation with one another, for one of its purposes was "to provide for a *more perfect union.*" Brownson argues therefore that if there had been no union or joint action whatsoever, " . . . it could not and would not have spoken of providing for a *more perfect union.*"[22]

In view of the fact that Brownson maintains that a convention does not institute or constitute society he maintains that the words "to provide for a more perfect union" should be interpreted to mean that the convention of 1787 recognized the fact that there were states, that these states had been acting jointly or in union with one another, and that it was necessary to provide a government which would express more perfectly the joint action which had always been present.

Brownson's case for an original union, however, is based primarily on the assertion that it was states acting jointly who declared independence and fought for it. It was states acting jointly who exercised and maintained that complete authority which is the distinctive characteristic of a sovereign.

In terms of Brownson's organic constitution this means that the fundamental germinal organization present in America was a unity in diversity — states and a union of states. This is the original organic constitution of the American Republic.

With the recognition of independence and the subsequent illegality of existing documents, this fundamental organization of the people remained. Consequently sovereignty passed to the states in union. Being invested with authority the organized people were authorized to enact legal documents. Being the act of a political sovereign, these documents are binding. They are the legitimate enactments of a sovereign.[23]

Thus far the basis on which Brownson expands his meaning of the constitution, both organic and written, has been established. Brownson's conception of its merits is a lofty one. Before proceeding with his exposition, it is necessary to discover the respective roles assigned to providence, and the statesmen whose philosophy he has berated in the formation of both the written and organic constitution.

First of all the elements from which the organic union of states developed — that is, the presence of colonies acting jointly — is not the product of human wisdom, foresight or deliberation. The organism called the union of states is providential, ". . . as much the work of Providence as the existence in the human body of the living solidarity of its members."[24]

Brownson does not hesitate to say that this union is the best possible system for the American people. Although it is the best it is not *mandatory* therefore that it should be supported:

> When we place the obligation to support our institutions on the notion we may have that they are the best, we give them only an intellectual basis, and can enlist only the intellect in their behalf; but when we demand obedience to them on the ground that they are the law, we base them on morality, and place them under the protection of religion. We demand then obedience as a *duty*, not merely as a sound judgment, and make loyalty not merely a sentiment, but a virtue.[25]

Although it may not appear such, Brownson's praise of the statesmen of 1787 is genuine. Their genius is to be found in the fact that they were, for the most part, guided by reality instead of their own speculations. They had the good sense to adopt existing institutions. To the extent that they were guided by reality they wrote well:

> The merit of the statesmen of 1787 is that they did not destroy or deface the work of Providence, but accepted it, and organized the government in harmony with the real order, the real elements given them. They suffered themselves in all their positive substantial work to be governed by reality, not by theories and speculations. In this they proved themselves statesmen, and their work survives.[26]

For a more thorough comprehension of Brownson's stand on these points it is now advisable to investigate his exposition in the *American Republic*. In it he maintains that the American Republic is the best practical solution of the problems confronting the political philosopher, not only with reference to the reconciliation of liberty and authority, but also to the problem of the relationship between church and state.

7

THE AMERICAN REPUBLIC

BROWNSON'S exposition of the nature of the American Republic is for him the most important part of his political philosophy. There is no complete authority except in the union of states. Consequently the American Republic is an organism whose immediate members are states. Thus individuals are members or the organism only inasmuch as they are members of states.

Since the people constituted a nation by the union of states are by that fact sovereign, they are authorized to institute government or to modify the existing government. It is their privilege as sovereign. In America the distinctive organ for the exercise of authority is the convention.[1]

It is quite obvious however, that for Brownson a convention called at random, appealing to the people as a consolidated mass irrespective of state organization, does not represent supreme political authority. He has just shown that the political people exist only as distributed into distinct but inseparable units. They have authority to ordain and institute government only as assembled through states in union with other states.

For Brownson, therefore, the traditional phrase "We the people of the United States" is very expressive. It places authority exactly where it is located: in the people of states united. The phrase "in convention jointly assembled" is also expressive because it indicates the distinctive organ through which the sovereign speaks and commissions the agencies whereby he exercises complete authority.

The convention is really the fundamental government of the country because it is the immediate organ of the sovereign. Thus the government of the country, as its sovereignty, is one and indivisible. The sovereign exercises his functions through two mediums, a general government and particular state governments.

This division of powers is according to Brownson distinctively American. It is found nowhere else in the world and is similar to no previously existing form of government. It is this distinctive feature which is the glory of the American system.[2] Thus it must be investigated more carefully.

First of all, the division of power is not between a national and a state government. This is to imply that one is the sovereign government while the other is subject, which is inadmissible because sovereignty passed to the states united. If one alone were sovereign, it would be the sole, complete government of the country. Therefore the governments are coordinate. The respective spheres of each are defined. They are both dependent upon the sovereign who instituted them, but not upon each other. Consequently each is supreme within its own sphere. The basis of division is more properly between a general government controlling all matters of common interest and a particular government having jurisdiction over the particular relations of individuals.[3] One must be careful to understand exactly what is meant by general and particular welfare:

> The private welfare of each is, no doubt, for the welfare of all, but not therefore is it the "General welfare," for what is private, particular in its nature, is not and cannot be general. To understand by general welfare that which is for the individual welfare of all or the greater number would be to claim for the general government all the powers of government, and to deny that very division of powers which

is the crowning merit of the American system. The general welfare, by the very force of the words themselves, means the common as distinguishable from the private or individual welfare.[4]

Understood in this way it is clear that the American system does not have its basis in a system of checks and balances which obstruct the exercise of power in order to guard against its abuses. There is a division of power itself rather than mutually antagonistic powers. There is no attempt to make forces collide, but there is an attempt to make them operate in different spheres in order to prevent collision. This provides for the exercise of power while at the same time it very obviously provides an effective check against the abuse of power or its excessive centralization. The general government cannot oppress the private rights of individuals because they are withdrawn from its jurisdiction. In regard to these the states themselves govern supremely.[5]

Furthermore, the particular state government cannot oppress the individual because the same division of power is carried on into the heart of the state itself. In some states, more than others, the division is carried on by means of counties, town corporations, cities and similar institutions, each of which is entrusted with the jurisdiction of affairs that are purely local. There is therefore little danger of excessive centralization of power within the state itself.

Understood in this way, the American system is unique. It has no exact prototype in any previously existing system. Referring to the English system of checks and balances he says:

> The principle of the British constitution is not the division of the powers of government, but the antagonism of estates, or rather of interests, trusting to obstructive influence of that antagonism to preserve the government from pure centralism. Hence the

study of the British statesman is to merge diverse and antagonistic parties and interests so as to gain the ability to act, which he can do only by intrigue, cajolery, bribery in one form or another, and corruption of every sort.[6]

Commenting upon what he believes to be its opposite, French imperialism, he says:

> The emperor confessedly holds his power by the grace of God and the will of the nation, which is a clear acknowledgment that the sovereignty vests in the French people as the French state; but the imperial constitution, which is the constitution of the government, not of the state, studies, while acknowledging the sovereignty of the people, to render it nugatory, by transferring it, under various subtle disguises, to the government, and practically to the emperor as chief of government.[7]

Brownson's purpose in introducing both the English and the French is to show that they represent extremes. The English system as he represents it guards against the abuse of power by obstructing its exercise on the basis of mutually antagonistic interests. He remarks that if these checks and balances were perfect, there would be no exercise of power whatsoever. Practically, however, it is not perfect. At one time certain interests combine to get the upper hand, while after a time possession is secured by other interests. Imperialism, on the other hand, tends to an excessive concentration of power.

The American system is represented as combining the best features of both and is consequently superior to either. It preserves unity without concentrating power. It provides for the exercise of power without setting up antagonistic interests to obstruct it.[8]

A further examination of this distinctive American system discloses the fact that "It is not a constitutional monarchy not a constitutional aristocracy, but, perhaps, may be defined, with sufficient accuracy, a constitutional democracy, although the terms are to us a little incongruous. We would, if the thing were possible, exclude the word democracy altogether, as unnecessary and apt to mislead."[9]

However Brownson remarks in the same place that it is apparently ". . . too late to get rid of the term." Consequently he takes the position that if people will insist upon adopting the term, he may as well tell them what their system means in terms of democracy. It is not, however, without a snort of scorn for the term itself that he makes this concession.

Brownson says that the only democracy compatible with American institutions is what he calls territorial democracy. It is this conception of territorial democracy based upon the theory of an original union that gives him some claim to originality as a political philosopher. It is consequently necessary to investigate it carefully, because it is for him the most important part of his analysis of the American Republic.[10]

Brownson states simply that American or territorial democracy means that the right to participate in the exercise of authority is derived from the territory:

> The great body of freemen have the elective franchise, but no one has it save in his state, his county, his town, his ward, his precinct. Out of the election district in which he is domiciled, a citizen of the United States has no more right to vote than has the citizen or subject of a foreign state.[11]

This statement merely means that the right to vote is not a personal right. Since it is not personal, it is not nomadic. Since a person cannot wander about, voting whenever and wherever he pleases, the political power which is represented by the vote cannot come from him as a person. It must be confined to or based upon a place or a territory.

BROWNSON ON DEMOCRACY

The doctrine that the right to vote is derived from territory is merely the particular application of a doctrine that has been established in Brownson's view on the origin of authority. In his analysis of the civil as opposed to the barbaric order, he has indicated that the state must be a *res publica*. Otherwise its authority is, and can be, only personal — a private right or privilege. Being personal it is therefore arbitrary, despotic in principle, and therefore illegitimate. It implies that man has dominion over man, which is inadmissible because all men are naturally equal.

Since the right to vote is the right to exercise political authority, it is erroneous, strictly speaking, to refer to it as a right, for political authority is, and can be, only a public trust. Being a trust, the extension of suffrage cannot be advocated on the ground that it is a natural right of men, or that it is the right of every person because he is a person.[12] It inheres in the *res publica* as an organism to be exercised for the welfare of the whole. Consequently the society called the state may extend or restrict suffrage in order to secure its own welfare. In the case of the American Republic, the organic people enacted written constitutions determining who may vote and the conditions upon which he may vote. Since these constitutions were enacted by an organic independent people who had the right to enact them, they are law.

The constitution, however, provides for its own amendment. Such amendments are of course legal if they are amended in the manner prescribed by the constitution. The political people determined by the constitution may extend or restrict suffrage if in their judgment it is for the best interests of society to do so.

In Brownson's estimation it would be illogical on the part of the American people to refuse, for example, to extend suffrage to negroes or to impose restrictions in terms of wealth.[13] The American Republic has in its radical constitution no elements of royalty, hereditary nobility, racial discrimination, or class distinction in terms of wealth. In addition, property has enough advantage in itself without making it a basis for voting.

He did not, however, advocate the indiscriminate extension of suffrage. Negroes, for example, should first prove themselves capable of maintaining themselves as free men before being entrusted with the ballot. He opposed, and one might add rather vehemently, the extension of suffrage to women on the ground that it would be to no one's advantage to permit them to enter the political arena:

> The very fact that woman is the weaker vessel ... renders her less morally independent, less frank, open and straightforward, and in a contest with man, compels her to resort to art, artifice, intrigue, in which alone she can equal or surpass him. Her accession to the political body should, therefore, only introduce an additional element of political and moral corruption.[14]

Besides that, man does not separate his own interests from those of women; consequently she cannot claim the privilege of voting on the ground that it is necessary to protect her own interests: "He always includes in his private interest that of some woman; and if he cheats, robs, steals, swindles, gives or takes bribes, it is almost always for the sake of his Eve, or at least for the sake of his family."[15]

This brief survey of Brownson's view of suffrage indicates that he was not opposed to the simple idea that the people should have a voice in the government. He maintains, however, that this voice in government must find expression only in and through the constitution. This constitution, it has been noted, is based upon distinct but inseparable units. The presence of these units rendered practical a system in which the power of government is decentralized without checks and balances to obstruct the exercise of power. In order to retain intact this desirable arrangement, Brownson contends that democracy must be continued on its territorial basis. Each state must continue to be attached to its own distinct territory, and to exercise authority over the affairs pertaining to it.[16]

Opposed to the conception of authority as attached to and inseparable from territory is the conception that it is attached to persons.[17] Such authority is essentially despotic. It gives power to govern without the right to govern. Its despotism is manifested either in individualism, or in humanitarianism or socialism.[18] Brownson believed that both of these trends were manifesting themselves in the political currents of the day.

While, theoretically, the trend toward personal or individualistic democracy, ending ultimately in anarchy, is as dangerous as humanitarian democracy, Brownson believed that the danger of an individualistic trend had been checked effectively by the civil war. There is no further danger that the union will be broken by the undue assumption of authority by the individual states: "The danger to American democracy from that quarter is forever removed, and democracy à la Rousseau has received a terrible defeat throughout the world, though as yet it is far from being aware of it."[19]

Brownson believed that the danger from the other quarter was much more imminent.[20] With the termination of the war he wrote that the Union victory would be interpreted as a victory for reformers fighting for social equality. Thus the movement for social reform would be stimulated temporarily at least throughout the world.[21] The pendulum would swing away from individualism and toward the other extreme.

Regarding its immediate effects in the United States he writes that the Union victory will result in a tendency toward humanitarianism or consolidation, both within individual states and among the states themselves. He notes however that "The constitution, in the distribution of the powers of government, provides the states severally with ample means to protect their individuality against the centralizing tendency of the general government, however strong it may be."[22]

He writes further, that along with the tendency to centralize power in the general government is the tendency to centralize it in the hands of the executive. States, he believed, would always retain their identity. But during the civil war it was necessary to confer almost dictatorial powers upon the president — powers he was unwilling to relinquish with the termination of the war: "The danger that the general government will usurp the right of the states is far less than the danger that the executive will usurp all the powers of congress and the judiciary."[23] Continuing, he says that "Congress clothed the president with dictatorial powers for war purposes only, but the executive forgets this."

It has been indicated in the discussion of the democratic theory that this centralizing tendency is inevitable, according to Brownson, if the proposition is defended, in simple unequivocal terms, that the people must rule, that they have the natural right to vote, that their *opinion* must be consulted on every issue. Such appeals are and can be made only to the people as a mass of individuals in which case they are no more sovereign than the people of a foreign state. Furthermore, the opinion to which appeals are made is in Brownson's estimation, seldom anything but a compound of ignorance, prejudice, passion, caprice, and interest, constantly varying, condemning a Socrates one day to drink hemlock, and the next erecting a temple to his memory.[24] This direct appeal to the people in their capacity as individuals is vicious. Representatives ask not, what is just, what is right, but what will my constituents say? Opinion is thus the ultimate criterion of right. This is political atheism.

In Brownson's estimation a society based upon the conception that people have the right to rule is based upon the falsehood that dominion over man is attached to man. The pendulum of such a society must swing from individualism to socialism, egoism to humanitarianism, anarchy to caesarism. American society cannot be attached to such a pendulum.

It is in opposition to this conception of authority that Brownson proposes his theory of territorial democracy. The people who are *the* political people are determined by the constitution, which is a law above the people because it is enacted by a sovereign. The constitution determines further the extent to which, and the conditions under which, the political people may function. Under that constitution authority is confined to a definite place. People acting through the constitution of the place are sovereign in it; they perform the functions of a sovereign by controlling domestic affairs. Any one not domiciled in it has no more authority in it than the resident of a foreign state. It is the people of distinct places acting jointly under the constitution who are the sovereign people. Thus territorial democracy is the only democracy compatible with both the organic and written constitutions of the American Republic.

Brownson admits that a conception of a people who are one and many is a difficult one. He admits that the conception of a territory which is one but nevertheless distinct is a difficult conception. It is a conception of a society that resembles, more closely than any other society, the Trinity. In these passages Brownson takes a very lofty view of the American Republic:

> God is the author and type of all created things: and all creatures, each in its order, imitates or copies the divine being, who is intrinsically Father, Son, and Holy Ghost . . . In the Holy Trinity is the principle and prototype of all society, and what is called the solidarity of the race is only the outward expression, or copy in the external order, of what theologians

term the circumincession of the three divine persons in the Godhead.

Now, human society, when it copies the divine essence and nature either in the distinction of persons alone, or in the unity alone, is sophistical, and wants the principle of all life and reality.

The English system which is based on antagonistic elements, on opposites, . . . copies the divine model in its distinctions alone, which, considered alone, are opposites and contraries. It denies, if Englishmen could see it, the unity of God. The French, or imperial system . . . denies the distinctions in the model, and copies only its unity, which is the supreme sophism called pantheism. The English system tends to pure individualism; the French to pure socialism or despotism, each endeavoring to suppress an element of the one living and indissoluble *TRUTH*.[25]

Brownson points out, of course, that the unity in diversity of the American system resembles more closely the model or prototype of society than either of the other systems. It is the original, inherent unity in diversity that rendered practical the division of power that is the distinctive feature of American republicanism:

The special merit of the American system is not in its democracy alone, as too many at home and abroad imagine; but along with its democracy in the division of powers of government between a general government and particular state governments, which are not antagonistic governments, for they act on different matters, and neither is or can be subordinated to the other.[26]

At this point one begins to wonder why Brownson has neglected throughout his discussion of the merits of American republicanism to introduce the religious factor. He has maintained that individual liberty and public authority cannot meet harmoniously without the presence of infallible authority to define their respective spheres. As a matter of fact, Brownson devotes a very small portion of his work to a discussion of the relationship between church and state in America.[27]

The reason for this is the fact that Brownson endeavors to show that the American Republic is based upon principles which are catholic, universal. It recognizes the supremacy of the spiritual order which is all that Brownson would ask of any state. He has maintained that the church and state are distinct; they derive authority through different channels. As external corporations they are distinct, each having its own function. Being distinct, they should not be intermingled, the one with the other.[28]

Brownson does not attempt to establish the fact that the founding fathers were favorable or unfavorable to Catholicity. It has been indicated already that the private opinions of the founding fathers are of no consequence whatsoever in determining what is and what is not. What they thought of the matter is a question that may be interesting, important to many people, but not so to Brownson.

He says that *de facto* many religious sects and denominations of one sort or another were present at the birth of the nation. As a matter of fact, however, none of these sects ". . . have been able to get their peculiarities incorporated into its constitutions or its laws."[29] Whatever reasons may be alleged to explain the fact, nothing that is narrow, sectarian, bigoted, has been incorporated into the constitution. The nation neither adopted nor recognized the merits of one religion as opposed to another. If any attempt were made now to establish a sect as the religion of the nation, it would only ". . . array all the other sects as well as the church herself against the government."[30]

Another fact is that the state professes to be founded on, and to recognize, rights which are above it, anterior to it; these are called the "rights of man," among which are the traditional "Life, liberty, and the pursuit of happiness." They are derived from God, as are all other rights. In recognizing, for all practical purposes, that these rights are above it, held independently of it, the state ". . . acknowledges in reality, if not in form, as its basis, as its very foundation, not only the independence, but the supremacy of the spiritual order."[31]

Brownson is endeavoring to show that the nation does not feel itself free to destroy this religion or that, to impose this or that sectarian view as obligatory. There is rather a practical recognition of the fact that it is obliged to respect and to protect equally the religious convictions of its citizens. Thus it protects Catholics in the exercise of their religion. It protects their property from violence just as it does that of any sect. It recognizes and protects the right of the church to form and to direct the conscience of her subjects, to speak freely and to exert whatever influence she is able to exert.[32]

The relations between the church and state in America are nearly normal in the estimation of Brownson. The fact that they are normal is evinced by the lack of treaties and concordats, which are needed only where there is an attempt on the part of the state to interfere with the church. He concedes that such concordats are necessary in other states, and if they were broken it could be interpreted to mean that the state could do whatever it pleased with the church, her property and the religious convictions of her citizens. The very fact that there are concordats shows that all is not well and that concessions must be exacted to remedy an evil. Such treaties are unnecessary in the United States because the conditions necessary for the church to exert her influence are already adopted in the constitution of the nation.

This arrangement, while practical nowhere else, is in itself better than any other conceivable arrangement for the church. If she is the official religion of a state, political and ecclesiastical affairs tend to be inextricably interwoven. Ecclesiastical appointments sometimes necessitate state clearance before becoming effective. Subsequently to appointment, clerics must devote considerable time to purely political affairs, thus rendering less effective their spiritual endeavors. Purely civil acts are sometimes attributed to the church as part of her policy. Existing and flourishing in a monarchy, she is viewed as favoring monarchical as opposed to republican forms. Being involved in political affairs she is to an extent dependent upon political powers in order to operate. To the extent that she is thus dependent, the state may and often does use her to promote its own ends.[33]

It is in opposition to this confusion that the American system depicted by Brownson stands out in clear contrast. The principles necessary for the church to exert her influence are adopted not by treaties or concordats, or by a mixture of civil and ecclesiastical powers, but in the constitution itself. There is no mutual antagonism or distrust requiring concordats to establish spheres of church and state. Thus Brownson says:

> Where there is nothing in the state hostile to the church, where she is free to act according to her own constitution and laws, and exercise her own discipline on her own spiritual subjects, civil enactments in her favor or against the sects may embarrass or impede her operations, but cannot aid her, for she can advance no further than she wins the hearts and convinces the understanding. A spiritual work can, in the nature of things, be effected only by spiritual means.[34]

The relations between the church and state are not normal in any other nation in the world because the American Republic is the only modern, civilized state that is grounded in reality — in the recognition of the fact that there are rights which it as a state cannot touch. It is, in a word, the only state which is so constituted that the state may trust the church and the church is free to work without the interference of the state.

> Such being the case, no sensible Catholic can imagine that the church needs any physical force against the sects ... What are called religious establishments are needed only where either the state is barbarous or the religion is sectarian. Where the state, in its intrinsic constitution, is in accordance with catholic principles, as it is in the United States, the church has all she needs or can receive.[35]

At this point Brownson's conception of church and state in America is more clearly defined. There is no separation in the sense that the state is above the church and feels free to do with her whatever pleases its fancy. They are separate as external governing bodies, which is good because an attempt to establish her by law would

> ... only weaken her as against the sects, place her in a false light, partially justify their hostility to her, render effective their declamations against her, mix her up unnecessarily with political changes, interests, and passions, and distract the attention of her ministers from their proper work as churchmen, and impose on them the duties of politicians and statesmen.[36]

Also at this point it is necessary to introduce his conception of the union of church and state. He says that although the church and state are separate as external governing bodies, they are "... united in the interior principles from which each derives its vitality and force. Their union is in the intrinsic unity of principle, and in the fact that, though moving in different spheres, each obeys one and the same divine law."[37]

This means that the American Republic is grounded

in the real order, in a concrete recognition of rights which are above it, superior to it, which represent a law which it cannot violate. These rights are based upon God's law. Since it is the purpose of the state to protect them, God's law is already embodied in the state itself. It is adopted in its constitution. Thus the church and the state are united by the fact that both recognize and obey one and the same law of God.

On this basis Brownson maintains that the atmosphere of American Republicanism is conducive to the spread of Catholicity. In imitating as it does in its own feeble way the Trinity itself, it conforms to the prototype of all society. It is thus based on the real order; it is not sectarian, copying its model only in its unity or diversity. It is catholic, universal. For the simple reason that they are sects, protestant denominations are out of joint with that which is universal. According to Brownson, they have "a . . . half avowed conviction" that they must unite, that they cannot sustain themselves in such an atmosphere. Thus "They hold conventions of delegates; they . . . form 'unions,' 'alliances,' and 'associations;' but, unhappily for their success, the *catholic* church does not originate in convention . . . confederated sects are something very different from a church inherently one and catholic."[38]

Since American republicanism is thus catholic, universal, the sects maintaining themselves in it are not on a basis of equality with the church. She is naturally superior to them, and a contest between them, especially in America, is not a contest between equals:

> In the United States false religions are legally as free as the true religion; but all false religions being one-sided, sophistical, uncatholic, are opposed by the principles of the state, which tend, by their silent but effective workings, to eliminate them.[39]

Before concluding the discussion it is necessary to restate

Brownson's position. He has endeavored to show that American republicanism represents a good solution to the problem of individual liberty in relation to public authority. Because it does so it also solves the problem of the normal relationship between the church and state. In still other terms, he means that it is because the state has recognized and preserved the rights of God it has, and can have, no quarrel with the church.

In order to clarify his thought, it is necessary to approach it from a slightly different viewpoint. It is necessary to repeat briefly his conception of individual rights as God's rights, and the natural law as God's command to respect the natural order. The natural order includes both the rights of the individual and the rights of society. Society is necessary and natural for man and man is naturally social; both hold rights from God. The first aspect of this thought is that the individual has rights which he holds independently of society. In the event it recognizes individual rights above it, superior to it, which it cannot violate, the state is obeying God's command to preserve the natural order which includes such rights. It is in reality, although not in form, obeying God's moral law. As long as it continues to obey it the church can have no quarrel with the state.

If, on the other hand, the state assumes jurisdiction over the conscience of the individual, it thereby disobeys God's moral law. The church as the divinely appointed custodian of that law is obliged to protect the individual who obeys it. Ecclesiastical authorities must intervene, by turning politicians, by extracting concordats, or in some other way, in order to secure the rights which individuals hold from God.

Such intervention is for Brownson abnormal rather than normal. Normally the church and the state are distinct. One cannot absorb the other. The church does not replace the state, render it unnecessary, superfluous. Nor is the contrary true. Each has a distinct function. The church and state mut be distinct but not separated. Separation means that the church has no place in the state. It means the complete independence of the state — absolutism.

Thus Brownson advocates neither a mixture nor a separation of church and state. The ideal is an intrinsic union of church and state based upon a mutual recognition and respect of God's command to preserve the rights He has given to individuals, along with their distinction as external governing bodies. Such distinction is practicable nowhere else in the world because nowhere else is there a state which obliges itself, in its own inherent constitution, to obey God's natural law. For that reason the church is obliged elsewhere to become involved in political affairs, because without such intervention her right to exert her influence within the state would not be recognized. But this is necessary only when the state is so barbarously constituted that she must supervise its administration " . . . in order to infuse some intelligence into civil matters, and to preserve her own rightful freedom and independence."[40]

Thus Brownson holds that the church and state in America are intrinsically united. Whether the founding fathers were aware of it or not, the constitution enacted is conducive to the spread of Catholicism. It does not restrict, conflict with, or hamper in any way, the spiritual mission of the church.

This brief summary, based upon Brownson's conception of law as the command of God to preserve the natural order, has been confined to the obligation of the state to preserve the natural order with respect to individuals. Since the natural order includes society, the same command of God obliges the individual to sustain society.

Applied specifically to America, this means that allegiance is a moral obligation. Loyalty is a duty; duty discharged is a virtue. The preservation of this society may be, and in Brownson's estimation is, for the best interests of all concerned. Yet Brownson is never more violent in his denunciation of democratic tendencies than in his denunciation of the "stupid journalists and pothouse politicians" who urge allegiance on the ground that the American Republic is the best. What is best, what is desirable, is no reason for allegiance. The obligation to sustain the republic is based upon God's command to preserve the natural order. Failure to fulfill the obligation to sustain it is a failure to obey God's law, which commands the preservation of society.[41]

Brownson asks of Catholics, not only that they remember their obligations as citizens, but also that they study the American constitution in the light of their own theology. Their theology enables them to comprehend the difficult "unity in diversity" which is the glory of American republicanism.[42]

On the basis of the conception that American republicanism embodies the elements necessary for the solution of the problem of individual liberty in relation to public authority, it is thereby in possession of the elements necessary to solve practically the problem of the relationship between the church and the state. It is well qualified to solve that problem. The following passage represents the essence of what Brownson has endeavored to say:

> The religious mission of the United States is not then to establish the church by external law, or to protect her by legal disabilities, pains, and penalties against the sects, however uncatholic they may be; but to maintain Catholic freedom, neither absorbing the state in the church nor the church in the state, but leaving each to move freely, according to its own nature, in the sphere assigned it in the eternal order of things.
>
> The effects of this mission of our country fully realized, would be to harmonize church and state, religion and politics, not by absorbing either in the other, or by obliterating the natural distinction between them, but by conforming both to the real or

divine order, which is supreme and immutable. It places the two powers in their normal relation, which has hitherto never been done, because hitherto there has never been a state normally constituted . . .

Whether the American people will prove faithful to their mission, and realize their destiny, or not, is known only to Him from whom nothing is hidden. Providence is free and leaves always a space for human free will. The American people can fail, and will fail, if they neglect the appointed means and conditions of success.[43]

8

DEMOCRACY AND THE DESTRUCTION OF AMERICAN INSTITUTIONS

I. Patriotism

DEMOCRACY has been associated with everything that is good, true and beautiful in government. The term therefore evokes responses that become extremely intense, thereby rendering most difficult the calm, rational discussion that disdains vulgar invective.

Intense feelings are of course desirable only if they are aroused by things that are genuinely valuable; divorced from intelligence they are vicious rather than virtuous. This is true even of the feelings ordinarily called good, such as maternal love and patriotism. A mother whose love is not guided by intelligence very frequently causes considerable harm to herself and to her children. All of us have observed the behavior patterns of the "spoiled child" developed by the narrow and exclusive attention of unreasoning parents. We know too that their good intentions unfortunately fail to counteract the natural consequences of their stupidity.

Patriotism too involves an emotion ordinarily called good simply because of its intensity. Divorced from reason it is vicious. Communists, for example, feel very intensely about their objectives. Their zeal is evinced in their willingness to make tremendous sacrifices to promulgate their principles. We do not sanction them simply because they are enthusiastic. We do not oppose them simply because their feelings are intense, or because they themselves mean well or think their own intentions are good. They are aroused about the wrong things and should therefore be opposed.

To strive simply to intensify feelings of love is then obviously stupid. To determine the things that are genuinely valuable and therefore worthy of intense responses is of considerably greater importance. This work of reason must precede emotion; otherwise the feeling itself is without merit.

Individuals who feel intensely are unfortunately unimpressed by rational discussion. All of us are aware of this as a result of many personal experiences. Obvious examples are individuals who dislike relatives-in-law. Logic cannot change such resentment to love.

Americans feel very intensely about democracy. Arguments proving that it is not worthy of an enthusiastic response are dismissed as un-American, because democracy and Americanism are assumed to be synonymous.

Brownson's analysis is the result of a lifetime of intensive study of both democracy and American institutions. His conclusion that democracy is destructive of everything essentially and distinctively American is contrary to popular prejudice, which exists also in our own generation. The energy of many Americans is misdirected if he is correct. Here as elsewhere good intentions do not counteract the natural consequences of stupidity.

The possibility that our institutions are due to something more than democracy should be considered rather seriously by anyone willing to concede that America is superior to other nations. Superiority is and must be caused by the possession of something lacking in other nations. Anything possessed in common with other nations cannot be responsible for elevating us above them.

If democracy is a cause capable of producing institutions which preserve basic personal rights such institutions should exist wherever people have deposed kings, kaisers and emperors. Since democracy has been tried elsewhere, the reason why it works here and nowhere else is obviously not democracy, but something radically different from it.

To attribute our superiority to democracy means that we are above other nations only because American voters in their wisdom and virtue have elevated to office, both federal and local, only men who excel in intelligence, integrity and patriotism the statesmen produced by other nations. Comparatively recent investigations substantiate what we already believed — that a fair percentage of our public servants are neither wise, virtuous nor intelligent. Their superiority or lack of it may be determined rather easily by observing the results of the agreements they have made with the representatives of foreign nations. Are we to believe that Wilson, Roosevelt and Truman always outwitted Orlando, Clemenceau, George, Stalin and Churchill?

The purpose of the remarks which follow is to show that Brownson is perhaps correct in asserting that personal liberty remains, not because of democracy, but because we are not yet wholly democratic; not on account of our superior executives and legislators, but despite their demonstrable inferiority to the leaders of other nations.

Our form of government is something completely new and better, incomprehensible to those who insist upon explaining it in terms of one of the simple forms, or combinations of them enumerated by Aristotle or St. Thomas. This form renders the so called "democratic" institutions workable. This is our most precious possession worthy of the most sincere and enthusiastic response. Genuine patriots interested in the well-being of America must understand the basic structure that makes the nation to be what it is. Their energy should be directed toward the preservation of this form.

II. The Organic Constitution

The term constitution is used in its primary sense to signify that which constitutes a thing or makes it to be what it is. More simply the primary constitution is that which gives anything its structure or puts it together so that it exists. The unifying factor of a people cannot be a written document because only a people with already existing organizations are capable of producing a written document labelled the constitution. A written document is produced by a people acting as a unit. Without a unifying factor they could not exist as a unit and therefore could not act as one. It is evident that the basic organizations of America existed prior to any written documents they themselves produced.

These fundamental organizations were not produced by the men we honor as founding fathers. Distinct political corporations which exercised some jurisdiction over affairs pertaining to their own territory existed prior to the founding fathers. Affairs affecting all of the colonies jointly, their relations among themselves and with foreign powers, were not under the jurisdiction of any single colony; this was not due to their will. The existence in America of distinct territorial units joined together by a power really distinct from any one of the particular political corporations was not the result of any human wisdom, ingenuity or foresight.

These units retained their identity and continued to be joined together. Their war for independence was waged together, not by any one colony. Continued cooperation was necessary for them to exist as an independent political power capable of fulfilling the obligations of a political sovereign, which means jurisdiction over both foreign and domestic affairs. In the words of John Quincy Adams:

It is not immaterial to remark, that the signers of the Declaration, though qualifying themselves as the Representatives of the United States of America, in general congress assembled, yet issue the Declaration, in the name and by the authority of the good people of the colonies — and they declare, not each of the separate colonies, but the United Colonies, free and independent states. The whole people declared the colonies in their united condition, of right, free and independent states.

... The independence of each separate state had never been declared of right. It never existed in fact.

It is evident then that the political power of the United States never existed in the people as a single consolidated mass. Nor did any single state ever succeed in exercising all of the functions of a political sovereign. The nation is so constituted that it exists neither as separate states nor as a consolidated mass of individuals.

The American people exist in distinct units called states, each of which has a structure and organization of its own. These states are joined together; they are distinct but cooperative units. Therefore the people as individuals are joined together and act together, as a unit, only because states act together.

No political people existed apart from state organizations. No state could begin to exist or continue to maintain itself without cooperation. The authority of the nation inheres in this structure, for without it there is no political people with the right to rule.

The genius of our founding fathers consists in their practical wisdom. They were guided by reality rather than by theories as to the structure most desirable for the nation. They squandered no energy attempting to destroy the distinct organizations which always existed. They did not persist in attempts to avoid cooperative action. Circumstances were such that joint action was necessary to fulfill the obligations which confronted them. We are grateful to them for not marring the work of providence.

III. Democracy and the Destruction of American Institutions

The term democracy is used in a variety of ways. Brownson used it to signify the theory that political power inheres in the people. They may exercise it directly or through representatives who obey their will.

Political power in a democracy is not consequent upon wealth, property, birth or anything else accidental to man. It belongs to him because he is human. It is a natural right. Since all are equal as men, each individual must possess equal opportunity to exercise political power. Democracy then advocates universal suffrage and eligibility. Unanimity is of course impossible, so majority rule is a characteristic of democracy. Political power belongs simply to the person, sovereignty inheres in the people as persons.

To speak of the right to vote as a natural right is vicious. If a vote belongs to a man he has a right to sell it as he does anything else he owns. Since such conduct is not sanctioned it is evident that we do not really believe that the vote belongs to the person.

If the power to vote is a natural right of man he holds it prior to and independently of any constitution. Political power on the contrary can neither exist nor be exercised apart from society. It has no meaning for man save as a member of society. Political power exists only because a community exists. Community means that which is common to or shared by many; a common thing is of course vastly different from the sum total of interests which are personal, private and particular. It must be a *res publica*, constituted by public, not private wealth.

The common thing or *res publica* possesses the political power. The commonwealth involves more than personality, because personality is of necessity private, never public, general or common. A factor other than personality is consequently necessary to constitute a people or to give them a structure as a commonwealth or a *res publica*. This factor is the territory held in common; it makes people exist as a commonwealth or a community.

The political power of the community inheres in that which is responsible for its existence as a *res publica*. Since this is territory commonly owned, the political power is territorial, never personal. It is owned by the community, not the person. Since it exists in the public thing, the community controls it, not the person. It must be used in the same way that it exists, by the community and for its well being.

The basic germinal organization on a territorial basis is given to the people, not made by them as we have shown in the case of the United States. Its development is due to circumstances most of which are completely beyond the control of individuals within the community.

This means then that our constitution as a people, namely the territory and the way we are fixed upon it so that we hold it jointly as an organized people — is not the result of our own energy either as individuals or a group. Since we did not make it we do not own it; we have no right to use it arbitrarily or capriciously. It must then be given to us by a power above and superior to us — God. He did not produce it supernaturally, but providentially; that is acting in and through second causes or creatures.

Since the basic constitution is something that the people do not own in their own name, they hold it as a trust from God. The real owner determines the conditions under which it may be used. An obvious illustration is the use of a car which belongs to someone else. The owner tells us to be careful because it is not ours to use or to abuse.

The American people may exercise political authority then only because God has given them a structure or a constitution that makes them exist as an organization, not a mere collection of individuals. The authority exists in the organizing principle that makes them a community. Acting as individuals outside of and independently of the God-given structure that unites them no one individual or group ever does or can have a right to rule.

Since our constitution is given to us by God it is above and superior to us. It imposes obligations upon us. The action of the people as a nation is therefore subject to the restrictions imposed upon them by their constitution which defines the limits beyond which the use of power is forbidden. We are obliged to respect it, to use it properly, not to abuse or damage it because we do not own it. Power exercised independently of it is might, not right.

In the United States then political authority is a trust given to the community to be used by the organized people for their well-being as a community. The people are organized into distinct political corporations joined together. They may exercise legitimate authority only in and through the organizations that give them a structure as a community.

Brownson's condemnation of the tendency to adopt the democratic theories of the nature of government, society and its authority is then understandable. Democracy asserts the right to rule as a personal right. If it is personal it may be used according to the unrestrained will, caprice or fancy of the person. It is then power detached from right and therefore despotic.

If the right to vote is a genuine right, it is held independently of any organizing factor called a constitution. It may be used whenever and wherever the person pleases because he is a person wherever he is, independently of organizations or constitutions. Since the people are sovereign simply as persons, their collective will is supreme. The constitution is not something above them imposing obligations upon them; they made it and are therefore superior to it because the maker is and must be superior to the creature that owes its existence to his activity. The supremacy of the popular will, however expressed, is simply barbarism, despotism or totalitarianism.

It seems rather evident then that constitutional government and popular government are contradictory and mutually exclusive alternatives. If we assert the supremacy of the constitution we cannot simultaneously assert the supremacy of the popular will — neither of any one person nor all of them collectively. No two individuals have the right to rule a third; nor have one hundred and fifty million a right as persons to rule a single man, woman or child. They have the power but not the right as persons. As persons all of them, individually and collectively are subject in their action to the organization imposed upon them by God. Without these organizations there is no right to rule. Political authority is not then a personal right; it is not a right at all. It is a grant given to individuals by the community that holds it as a trust. The community has the obligation not to extend it to those unable to use it for the well being of the community. The community is not depriving any one of a right when it refuses to permit him to share in that which it holds as a trust from God.

A choice in favor of democracy means a willingness to repudiate constitutional rule. It is difficult to understand how it is possible for both the popular will as such and the constitution to be supreme at the same time. If one is supreme and sovereign the other is obviously inferior and subject. The supremacy of the popular will means that the constitution is the product of the people in their collective capacity. In order to give themselves a constitution they would of course have to act as a people before they exist as such. The constitution made by the people is a creature — different from the creator, inferior to it as is a chair, car or anything else made by him. His creature cannot bind him or impose any obligation upon him. It is just as plausible to contend that the tables, chairs and other things man produces are above him, superior to him, directing his conduct. He owes them neither allegiance nor respect. They are his to destroy if it pleases his will to do so.

Democracy then renders the repudiation of the constitution inevitable. If the right to rule is personal, not territorial, its use is authorized independently of particular political corporations called states, cities, counties, townships and villages.

Brownson proclaimed more than a century ago that the trend toward the centralization of political power is inevitable on democratic principles. One man or group of men is sufficient to ascertain and to express the will of a single consolidated mass of sovereign individuals. The government in Washington instead of being a general government whose jurisdiction is confined to general interests becomes a national government, or a government of the whole nation. Particular political corporations are no longer viewed as powers equal in every way to the general government, but different because exercised in a different place. They become unimportant; even those who teach government as a science in universities urge their elimination on grounds of inefficiency. On democratic principles anything more than a single man to express the will of a single consolidated mass is inefficient.

Those interested in determining for themselves whether or not the analysis of Brownson made a century ago is correct are advised to study carefully the investigations made by the Kefauver committee. It indicates clearly that the citizens of an area with jurisdiction over their own domain have not maintained governments strong enough to fulfill the obligations of government. Since society cannot continue to exist without government, the intervention of the general government is in direct proportion to the failure of local government. The corruption of local government, inevitable here on democratic principles, means the transfer of increasingly greater power to Washington.

When this occurs government of necessity involves graft, corruption, hypocrisy and deceit. On democratic principles those whom we send to Washington must represent the will of the sovereign who sent him. He will be obliged to secure a proportionate share of public funds for the benefit of his constituents. No matter what sort of a project for the area is proposed, representatives of other areas perhaps thousands of miles away have no reason whatsoever to be concerned with it. It is of no advantage to them or their constituents. Yet the majority of the whole is necessary to secure action of any kind. It is difficult then to understand how the necessary majority may be attained without the trading of votes. If then the general government becomes at all concerned with particular interests, or the sum total of particular interests, a stalemate would always be inevitable unless votes were traded: support the project which pleases my constituents and I will support yours.

The nation as a whole or a unit is then left without a government, for the primary concern of the representative becomes the particular interests. Whether or not the expenditures of the general funds are advantageous to the nation as a whole is the primary concern of no one.

Suppose for example that a dam in a state involves an expenditure of a million dollars. An individual campaigning in the area asserts bluntly that the project will augment the bank accounts of individuals in the area and provide them with conveniences, but that the expenditure is out of proportion to the value received by the nation as a whole. Suppose he asserts truthfully that his primary concern is the whole, not one of its parts, and that the general well being of the community is more important to him than their bank accounts. This would not of course increase his popularity.

His opponent on the contrary flatters his constituents,

defers to their wishes, tells them that their will is his command, and the only law that he consults. The sovereign people, convinced that their will is supreme cannot be expected to tolerate insubordination from a simple agent bound by their wishes and nothing else.

The government in Washington was of course designed so that its jurisdiction was confined to interests of their very nature general, common or universal. If this means the sum total of interests essentially particular it is of course the only government. Particular things are particular and remain that way no matter how many are gathered together. We compel representatives to place particular interests first, thus hastening the destruction of our distinctively American solution of the problems of government.

If then the jurisdiction of the general government is confined to general interests, the primary concern of everyone sent to Washington is the nation as a unit. The trading of votes necessary to secure the approval of a majority for projects beneficial to particular interests and areas would be reduced to a minimum.

A more important consideration concerns the primacy of the moral law. It is just as real, but different from sensible objects. It is never broken, but it wrecks individuals and nations who try to break it. No solution of any problem is possible without it. Brownson insisted upon its primacy. His failure to arouse the interests of individuals, particularly Catholics, in the constitution and its relation to the moral law was rather distressing to him. In his opinion, already cited, God did not work miracles to counteract the stupidity of individuals even though they are moral as persons. It was rather difficult for him to understand then how it would be possible for an individual to insist upon truth, honesty and justice in government while simultaneously insisting upon democracy and the necessity of obedience to the popular will. Democracy intensifies the causes responsible for the lack of morality. To insist upon both the primacy of the moral law and the popular will is hardly consistent.

The example already cited, of a federal project in a particular area, illustrates the fact that the adoption of democratic principles means that those who tell the truth will be removed from office. Similar examples may be multiplied indefinitely. A candidate for election in an area both anti-Catholic and anti-negro, for example, is in no position to tell the sovereign people that he will not obey their will; that the constitution does not favor any set of convictions about God, and that those who believe that God should be included in schools have a just claim to any funds, whether national or local, even though they are Catholic. He cannot state that democracy means equality, and that there is none if anyone is either inferior or superior to anyone else. Therefore not a single one of them is a whit better than any negro; that he will exert influence to make the equality a reality instead of a theory.

The emphasis on popular opinion as Brownson has shown means a rejection of both the constitution and the moral law. There is no open and avowed rebellion against either; both are ignored, which is far worse. Good is assumed to be that which pleases the will of the sovereign which is, in democracy, the popular will. The truth is that the moral law is supreme. The people in their collective capacity are subordinated to the constitution. The popular will is not sovereign. The subordination, not the supremacy of the popular will must be emphasized to maintain the supremacy of morality.

It would of course require a volume considerably larger than this one to apply the principles established by Brownson to the problems confronting us today. We will select three of them simply to illustrate the position of Brownson.

1. *Civil Rights.* There are no political people with the right to rule independently of state organizations. These particular political corporations determine to whom the

right to vote is to be given and the conditions under which it may be exercised. Citizens of other states have no more right to determine it than citizens of Germany or England.

A people aware of the nature of their own organizations could not ratify an amendment compelling any state to change the conditions under which it permits anyone to vote. As Brownson indicates, even the thirteenth, fourteenth and fifteenth amendments were not constitutionally adopted. If the rebellious states were outside of the union and not on a par with others, they could not rightfully ratify an amendment, for the constitution requires ratification by states within the union. If they were in the union on a par with the others, the federal government had no right to compel them to vote one way rather than another as a condition for readmission. Decisions concerning the conditions under which the privilege of voting may be exercised must remain within the jurisdiction of the state if we are to continue to have people organized into states and then united or joined together through state organizations.

2. *Income tax.* The sixteenth amendment authorizing the federal government to tax directly the income of individuals is a serious modification of our own organizations. It is one of the many steps taken by a people who confuse their own complex organization or form with that of a simple democracy, toward the destruction of their own internal organizations which they are obliged to keep intact. Individuals and their income are personal, not general or common. The sum total of their income remains personal; something common or general is not the result of anything essentially singular.

The ultimate effect upon the nation of this amendment cannot as yet be determined. On Brownson's principles the activities of the general government must increase as increasingly greater proportions of the tax dollar is gathered by Washington rather than local governing bodies. There appears to be a direct relationship between this amendment and the decrease in the power, importance and activity of local government. And since it gives the government direct power over the individual its tendency to confuse the general welfare with the sum total of particular interests increases. Instead of using the energy, initiative, resourcefulness and intelligence within an area to solve problems that affect it, the tendency seems to be toward exerting political pressure to secure federal aid.

3. *Personal liberty*. Americans value personal liberty; they are intensely concerned about it. No people are more ignorant of the means necessary to sustain it.

No creature has a right unless another creature has an obligation. I could not for example have a right to own a car and to use it unless that right imposed upon others the obligation to respect my claim. If then every individual within a nation is to remain in the possession of rights that God really gave to him, his claim imposes obligation upon the people in their collective capacity. Unless the people as a group, a nation or a unit have obligations, no individual does or can have a claim to anything, even his life.

If the people are sovereign, as the democratic principle asserts, they can do as they please. Their freedom to do as they please means that individuals as such have obligations, but no rights. The emphasis upon the freedom of the people means that they are under no obligations. To call them sovereign is to remove any restrictions upon their will however expressed. Precisely in so far as anyone is sovereign he is above all else; a sovereign as such cannot be subject. In so far as anyone is subject we call him not sovereign or government, but governed, restricted or subject. Individual liberty is assured then only by emphasis upon the subjection of the nation to a power above it.

The preservation of individual liberty means moreover that the differences between individuals must be preserved. To the extent that there is uniformity, there is no individuality. A real union means that there is a composite of things which retain their identity. It is difficult for anyone interested in personal liberty to contend for uniformity. To say, for example, that unless every worker makes shoes, nothing but shoes, of the same quality and size, there is no uniformity, is of course true. Whether or not uniformity is desirable is another question. One may contend that unless every student in every school is taught exactly the same at the same time, there is no uniformity. If such uniformity is desirable, the difference between individuals, their respective capacities, attitudes toward God as well as everything else individual about them, must be eliminated.

Brownson was of course ridiculed in his own day when he maintained that the destruction of liberty is inevitable if we become a democracy. Democracy means that the right to vote is a personal right. Political power must exist equally in every individual because everyone as a person is equal to every one else.

Equality of political power means social equality. An individual who has little money, no ability to organize or to persuade others, cannot exert as much influence in government as those more gifted. If then political equality becomes a goal worth attaining there is a movement toward the reformation of society. It cannot stop with the simple right to cast a vote because the desires that inaugurated the reform remain unfulfilled. It extends to society itself. It cannot stop until there is uniformity. There is no uniformity if one remains an individual, superior to some and inferior to others. Therefore heads protruding above the common level, whether in wealth, power or prestige, must be lopped off. This is done by making them all equally parts of the state — simple cogs in a wheel with no destiny of their own.

As Brownson has shown, the structure given to us as a nation, with the division of power on a territorial basis, with a respect for the differences between individuals and the desirability of protecting them embedded in our living constitution, with a respect for moral law to which we have pledged our subjection as a nation forming a part of our tradition, represents a completely new solution of the problems of government. Our solution, if rightly understood, will enable us to avoid both anarchy and totalitarianism.

IV. Church and State

Catholics, Protestants and Jews in America enjoy a larger liberty than they have ever known anywhere else in the world. Yet our nation has established no religion; it has no treaties, concordats or agreements with representatives of any organized religion.

We are confronted again with a fact that has a cause. Those desirous of maintaining the harmonious relationship existing between the church and state in America will endeavor to discover the principles from which it proceeds. Our conception of these principles is important because it determines the decisions we make in regard to practical problems which confront us, particularly in regard to the educational institutions established by religious groups. A failure to understand the principles involved will result in decisions detrimental to the well being of every religious group.

Brownson's analysis is not confined to the opinions of the founding fathers. We have seen already that they possessed great practical wisdom. They willingly abandoned ideas not in conformity with the reality that confronted them, in this case diverse groups professing a wide variety of beliefs. The lack of uniformity rendered the special recognition of one religion impracticable. Instead of attempting to secure uniformity in religion, they agreed to protect equally the right of conscience in all individuals. The compromise resulting in a pledge never to interfere with the religious obligations of any group was the only alternative. This again was simple recognition of an existing reality. The respect for religion was already part of the living tradition of the people. It became part of the written document of the people.

The full freedom and independence of religion was recognized when America acknowledged its incompetence in things spiritual. Permission to appoint ecclesiastical authorities, to teach this or that doctrine is neither asked nor given. Ministers of religion are free to devote all of their energy to the attainment of their primary objective. Freedom from the intervention of the state is recognized as a right, a just claim rather than a grant revocable at will.

This recognition of the difference and distinction between church and state is normal and natural. There is a difference between the civil and the ecclesiastical, the temporal and the spiritual. Since the church is and ought to be different from the state each should exist and operate as a really distinct corporation.

Nations failing to acknowledge a difference between the temporal and spiritual are abnormal. They refuse to recognize a difference between things as distinct as a man and a post. A nation which mixes the civil and the ecclesiastical is consequently abnormal. Nations which establish a religion, control the appointment of ecclesiastical authorities and feel qualified to render decisions in matters of faith are abnormal.

A nation which uses its power to establish a religion owns it, for the maker of a thing is its owner. The religion resulting from the exercise of state power belongs to the state. The state which owns a religion has not only the power but also the right to control it. No nation realizing that its power is restricted to the temporal order would feel competent to establish and control a spiritual reality. Such states attempt to perform functions really beyond their power. They have delusions of grandeur.

Since America owns no religion because it refused to

establish one, it refuses to act as though it had the right to control all religions. Since religion is not under the control of the state, it is obviously above the state, for the state controls that which is subject to it. The constitution incorporating a recognition of the supernatural order as above it, superior to its own power, and beyond its control is doing what every normal state should do.

Brownson expressed this view in terms of a union of church and state rather than a separation or a divorce. His expression is accurate because we must recall that union and uniformity or sameness are entirely different. Sameness cannot be union because there are no different realities to be combined. We cannot for example maintain that there is no union in an individual because he has both arms and legs. To contend for a union of church and state is to maintain first of all that they are different and that they must continue to remain different and distinct corporations. A union means that the church and state will not be mixed or confused any more than an arm will become a leg because both are parts of a whole.

Union implies not only difference but also togetherness. To contend for the union of church and state means that they must continue to exist together and to cooperate. This is necessary because neither one by itself can supply everything necessary to satisfy man's needs. To separate them means that they can no longer exist and act in the same place. One must exclude the other. For the state to exclude religion means that it can supply everything that man needs. There is then nothing beyond itself that can be a good for man. Separation cannot be part of the American tradition because we have always recognized the spiritual needs of man as genuine needs which he has a right to attain.

The union between the church and state in America is actual and real, but is is internal rather than external.

Visible symbols such as treaties and concordats with spiritual powers signify the presence of discord rather than harmony. They are necessary only when the state interferes with the right of the individual to attain a goal beyond the state. The obligation of the state to respect this right is incorporated in the living traditions of America as well as its written constitution. Concordats will be necessary only if and when the nation violates the right of the individual to practice his religion.

When the nation recognizes the right of God's church to form the conscience of those who acknowledge its authority it is obeying the law of God. This is all that can be asked of it. If God had authorized nations to exercise jurisdiction also over the supernatural order He would operate in them as He does in His church. This would of course render religion superfluous.

The doctrine of the separation of the church and the state leads then to their confusion and identity. If there is no destiny for the individual beyond the state, the state is the end of man. This means that man is for the state: there is nothing beyond it that he can reach. Religion is then unnecessary. The state is the only religion. It means that the state and religion are one and the same. This is the confusion or identity of church and state, not their union. If on the contrary man is not for the state but for something beyond it, the state is obliged to protect the individual in his efforts to attain his goal. There is then a union of church and state because they both work together in the same domain.

V. Private and Public Schools

Catholic periodicals invariably incorporate commentaries on political policies affecting parochial schools. Many of them are prompted by discussions regarding the transportation of children attending such schools or the constitutionality of federal aid to schools maintained by religious organizations.

One rather distressing aspect of such discussions is the failure to clarify the basic issues involved. In objecting to discrimination against parochial schools we assume, perhaps unconsciously, that the distribution of public funds to schools making no provision for teaching religion of any kind is compatible with the constitution. Such aid is clearly and explicitly contradicted by the constitution itself. Yet the position of those who boldly assume the contrary remains unchallenged.

The conception that a nation cannot at one and the same time take a stand favoring both of two mutually exclusive and contradictory alternatives is rather simple. It cannot for example pledge itself to protect the right to life while protecting and even rewarding those who destroy life. If therefore the nation does as a matter of fact pledge itself to protect the right to worship God it cannot at the same time penalize individuals for exercising that right, nor can it reward either atheism or agnosticism.

Whether or not a nation should adopt a constitution which prefers theism to atheism, or the converse, or should remain neutral, is beside the point at issue. What might have been done is no doubt interesting but unimportant.

Communism, for example, is and must be atheistic. Being both atheistic and consistent it cannot penalize individuals simply because they are atheists; nor can it reward them because they are theistic. If it takes a stand in favor of atheism and against theism it will penalize theists. The gross absurdity of a contrary position is apparent.

There is of course considerable evidence to indicate that our constitution is not neutral but avowedly pro-Christian. To maintain the contrary is difficult for anyone who has read the Declaration of Independence or the Constitution, or has looked at any American coin or taken an oath in court.

It is moreover a simple and obvious fact that the constitution which explicitly protects the right to worship God does not explicitly acknowledge a right to deny, to reject or to exclude God. An interpretation suggesting that those protected by the fundamental law of the land should be penalized while those who enjoy no such explicit recognition are deserving of a rich reward is obviously absurd.

Yet individuals whose conscience forbids them to send their children to institutions which make no provision for including instruction in religion are not equal to those who have no such convictions. In a village in Illinois, for example, 879 children attend the parochial schools. The annual cost of educating these children in the public schools exceeds $360, excluding the cost of the buildings, depreciation, interest on indebtedness, etc.

It requires no mathematical genius to discover that the Catholics of the village pay an annual tribute exceeding $300,000 to exercise a right reputedly recognized and guaranteed by the fundamental law of the land. They are required by law to pay taxes to support the educational institutions of those with no convictions. The same situation prevails in other communities.

A constitution which is pro-theistic must of necessity be anti-atheistic. There would then be greater harmony between actual practice and the spirit as well as the letter of the constitution if the nation required those desirous of excluding religion to organize and to maintain their own educational institutions at their own expense.

The most common objection to such a proposal is based upon the alleged neutrality of the state in regard to religious organizations. Because of their diversity and because the constitution forbids discrimination in favor of any particular group, a system making no provision for any religion is the only practical solution. We do not recall that the founding fathers decided that because there were so many different religions in America it was necessary to exclude all of them or to penalize all equally. It seems preciously close to a contradiction to identify equal protection and freedom for all religions with the exclusion of religion. Nor is a system which restricts public funds accumulated by taxing all individuals to those who consent to exclude religion, in any way neutral. To maintain that a solution which excludes Christ is the only one that can be devised by a Christian nation is a rather sad commentary on the intelligence of Christians.

The neutrality of the nation in regard to religion means that the nation cannot identify itself with a particular religion nor can it identify itself with the absence of religion or anything contrary to religion. To distribute public funds equally on the basis of enrollment to any organization willing to undertake the task of educating children without depriving them of religious instruction is not to impair the neutrality of the nation.

As a matter of fact there would be only three kinds of institutions — Jewish, Protestant and Catholic. Protestants generally defend the opinion that one religion is practically equivalent to another. This is only the logical consequence of the Protestant principle of private interpretation. If it is true that the Holy Spirit directly enlightens each individual who reads the bible with the proper dispositions, one opinion must be as good as another because the Holy Spirit guarantees the truth of each view. Thus we read each Sunday of ministers exchanging pulpits. There should then be little or no difficulty in agreeing upon the instruction to be given in the classroom. Since no minister would elevate himself above the Holy Spirit he would be most careful to refrain from foisting his interpretation upon one whom the Holy Spirit Himself enlightens.

If such a policy were to result in the multiplication of educational institutions by religious organizations there would be at least the possibility of stemming the decline of morality which so many decry. A generation of children so educated would have at least an elementary knowledge of God without Whom there can be no moral law, and of the moral law itself without which the nation cannot endure.

Secondly the cost of education would decline thereby alleviating an already staggering burden. To support an orphan in a public institution in the state of Illinois costs approximately $3023.00 annually; private institutions receive $300.00 for rendering the same service. It would seem reasonable therefore to anticipate a proportionate decrease in the cost of education by private organizations.

Thirdly, such a policy would guard effectively against the spread of "statism," a primary concern today. At least a generation would learn that the creator has endowed us with certain inalienable rights; that since these rights are anterior to the state, they can not be violated. Individuals so instructed should resent and oppose any attempts to suppress them.

A clarification of the position defended thus far requires a restatement of the traditional policy of neutrality in regard to religious convictions. It is sometimes interpreted to mean that the nation will not identify itself with any particular viewpoint on the ultimate origin and destiny of man and the universe. Thus the conviction that little or nothing can be known about God is just as sincere a conviction as its contradictory and is therefore deserving of recognition because the nation respects the right of conscience equally in all individuals.

The obvious reply is that agnosticism is either the contradiction of that which is protected in the constitution or it is itself a religion. If it is the contradiction of religion it is not and cannot be protected without amending the constitution.

If on the other hand it is a religion we should not forget that there shall be no laws respecting it. As a particular religion it can claim no more recognition than any other conviction.

In this case those protected by the constitution may be divided into two groups: those who feel that educational institutions should provide instruction in religion and those who feel that there should be no such instruction. The traditional policy of neutrality, if it means anything at all, must mean that national policy should favor neither viewpoint. Under the present policy agnosticism claims protection as a religion while receiving special recognition because it is not a religion.

The nation was not founded for the protection and propagation of agnosticism, nor of the Christianity which excludes Christ. It should not be impossible therefore to show that those opposed to religious instruction in schools have no exclusive claim to public funds.

The most amazing aspect of the existing situation is the fact that Catholics are sometimes grovelling, subservient and apologetic in the face of those whose position violates justice as well as common sense and the constitution. As Catholics we should reject our defensive attitude; as worshippers of God we should assume a justifiably aggressive stand — one that finds its legal and logical support in the constitution.

VI. World Government

No lengthy discussion is necessary to indicate the intrinsic absurdity of attempts to establish any sort of a United Nations, United States of Europe or World Government. That society and government cannot be created has been amply demonstrated throughout the body of the book. That which results from the activity of an individual or a nation is a creature. It could not exist, much less act, unless nations gave existence to it. The power it has is not its own. The sovereign giving power to a creature gives it to him as his agent revocable at his will.

Government on the contrary means authority exercised over subjects who have the obligation of obedience. To call an agent with no power of its own government is simply a violation of common sense. If it has no power of its own it is not above the sovereign which has such power. If it is not above its creator it cannot command him and compel obedience. It cannot then be government. Yet the advocates of world government seriously expect a creature with no power of its own to act as though it were above the creator, superior to him and capable of directing his conduct. It is more sensible to mantain that the car produced by human energy should drive the man and direct him to his destination.

An agent created by many different nations with obviously different and conflicting interests reputedly acts as the representative of all of them. Yet if any two nations have different aims and therefore conflicting interests, the agent cannot avoid actions detrimental to one and advantageous to the other. An optimist may hope that a nation will give its agent power to frustrate its own objectives; he may hope too that criminals will eventually hang themselves to save the expense of a trial and that business corporations will appoint agents authorized to bankrupt them.

Democracy is again the basic error responsible for the absurdity of placing the creatures above the creator. It supposes that sovereign individuals or nations create society and government by agreeing to surrender some of their rights and to keep others. In discussing the contract theory of government we have shown that sovereignty is surrendered in its entirety or else none at all is surrendered. This theory maintains that man's nature as a social animal is the result of his free decision to become a kind of a thing that he is. The social nature of man is given to him; without it he doesn't exist and it seems rather evident that without existence he cannot act.

Assuming the truth of the democratic theory, we maintain that a written document is sufficient to constitute a people and make them exist as a unit independently of any habits, customs and traditions that have put them together in a particular way. Every one of the individuals supposedly united in this way needs only a vote that he can use as he pleases and he has everything necessary to protect himself. It is like supposing that if each one had one hundred dollars to begin with, and no one had more than that, the money would remain equally divided if only all were left free to do what they pleased. Where everyone is left free, subject to no authority the money gravitates toward the most powerful and unscrupulous gangsters in the areas. The same is of course true of political power. That is why nations which are changed into democracies by benevolent foreign powers become totalitarian. If the democratic theory of society and government is false it is difficult to understand how a foreign policy based upon it can do anything except intensify and prolong the existing chaotic situation.

The establishment of government is nonsense because all of the government necessary to preserve peace already exists. God has given it to us. We have seen that none of it is given to a person as such. All persons, individuals and groups are subject to commonwealths He has established, not directly, but through creatures called second causes. Nations then are not sovereign, but subject to His law. Some of them have of course abused their organizations. They have acted as though they were not subject, but sovereign as a people with the complete freedom to do what they pleased.

The rejection of morality means that there is no appeal

to right to direct conduct. If then right is rejected, might is the only alternative. Violence is inevitable.

For nations to recognize the moral law means that they acknowledge the real existence of something different from themselves to which they must conform their conduct. It imposes obligations which bind them. The law is of course moral, not physical. This means that its acceptance must be voluntary, but the failure to accept it will result in violence damaging everyone concerned.

If no such law exists, no nation can be really right and none wrong. If it does exist individuals or nations contradicting its enactments are wrong. Anyone asserting that the conduct of any nation is morally wrong must then concede the reality of such a law.

If God made such a law He also had the good sense to authorize a court of competent jurisdiction. The founding fathers wrote a relatively simple document called the constitution; they were intelligent enough not to add that each individual is authorized to declare whether or not his own action is permitted or forbidden by it. They were not democratic enough to decide that each individual is bound only by his own interpretation of it. Catholics insist that God is as intelligent as the founding fathers.

To permit each individual to determine the content of the law, whether or not he himself has violated it and whether the violation deserves a penalty is to render the law innocuous. I am not bound by the speed laws if it is within my power to judge whether or not to permit an officer to arrest me or the judge to impose a penalty. A law without a court to determine whether or not it has been violated is not a law simply because it is not above the individual.

Atheists of course hold that there is no God and no law, and most Protestants maintain that the individual himself judges what it means and how to apply it. Catholics hold that God has established an organization; it does not of course make God's law; it simply declares what it is, and what actions violate it. Infallibility is not the personal right of individuals. God Himself works in and through this organization, but not in the same way that He operates to establish the social structures of man.

As already indicated His moral law which binds all creatures is different from a physical law but just as real. Because we are moral agents He expects us to accept it and to conform to it. According to Brownson at least, He does not therefore expect the state to use physical force to compel individuals to accept His church. The function of the state is simply to maintain conditions which permit the full freedom of the individual to accept it and to fulfill the obligations it imposes. When it does that much it fulfills its obligations as a state.

On Brownson's principles God's law is prior to all else. Creatures are required to recognize its primacy. The state must act as though its first and most important obligation is to be just. If in addition sufficiently large numbers of those representing states acknowledge a single spiritual authority, arbitration rendering recourse to violence unnecessary is at least possible.

Submission to spiritual authority is of its nature voluntary. Because Brownson believed that states everywhere adopted the democratic doctrine of absolute supremacy, he expected no such voluntary submission.

On Brownson's principles the nations of Europe cannot give themselves a new social structure. Existing structures are destroyed only by external force. Thus the rebellion against the only real power above the nation results in violence, which may in turn cause the death of existing nations. The remaining remnants will be united by reason of circumstances. The society thus formed will then authorize agents to rule.

Brownson then saw that a government for the universe

already exists. The sovereign people refuse to recognize it. They cannot really break the law, but attempts to do so will wreck them, as much so as their failure to acknowledge the reality of a law of gravity. Since they deem themselves sovereign and therefore dissatisfied with God's government they attempt to create one flexible to their will. Their attempts must fail because nations are not God. The violence ensuing from their stupidity is a terrible price to pay to keep up the dignity and majesty of their Godship.

9

CONCLUSION

THAT trends toward communism and the destruction of personal freedom would be intensified in every community on earth was for Brownson a prediction as obviously true as a forecast that men would continue to eat. He appreciated the presence of a driving force far more powerful than the desire for food. People are convinced that democracy is a reality which satiates this deeply rooted craving, and therefore accept it without reservation.

The human appetite in question is described as a desire for unlimited power; a tendency toward superiority for its own sake; a mass rebellion against restrictions as such. People make themselves God; everything and everyone including God must bow to their omnipotent will.

Brownson observed its manifestation in both individuals and groups. It appears when individuals make their own conception of right absolute. Examples are communists demanding protection for a right to destroy the community. Their arbitrary exercise of power is labelled liberty and authority obliged to interfere with it is declared despotic. Business corporations, labor organizations and particularly agricultural interests act on the same principle when their power is used to coerce the community to pay excessively for goods and services, even when the existence of the community is endangered. They elevate themselves above the community, using it as a means to promote selfish interests

CONCLUSION

and insist upon acting as though there is no real right to which their own conceptions must conform.

Individuals cannot help acting that way when democracy convinces them that the right to rule is their personal property and that their personal approval alone suffices to render any rule rightful. Individuals who identfy right with their own will are absolute. The people as democracy depicts them are creators; they feel capable of making the whole of society without using any previously existing material. Democracy tells them they are God; they believe it, and without wounding their orthodoxy or shocking their piety. The ultimate result of conduct stemming from such beliefs is anarchy. Society cannot sanction it and continue to exist. A clash between individuals and society exists as soon as it begins. Brownson recognized society as the more powerful contestant. It would attribute to itself the right to exercise power without limit. He was then concerned with its manifestations in the community.

Sovereigns are subject to no restrictions whereas creatures are, and must forever remain, restricted. Those aware of their status acknowledge their limitations. Those aiming simply at the removal of restrictions obviously forget their status as creatures. A society whose conduct results in the destruction of restraints deifies itself. The trend to deify society is evident to anyone who observes our conduct as a nation. The examples which follow are selected to illustrate its existence; they may be multiplied indefinitely.

1) We speak of our nation in terms of self-government. Self-government is an obvious contradiction. A prisoner who locks himself in a cell is not confined if he keeps the key. A nation confined only by its own restrictions is like the prisoner who makes his own cell and key. Both may piously pretend that they cannot free themselves when they please, but neither is really restricted. Names signify things. A nation aiming at self-government aims at the removal of restraints, pious platitudes to the contrary notwithstanding.

CONCLUSION

We recognized real restraints only when we recognized the key as another's possession.

2) To prate of subjection to law while retaining the right to judge infractions is absurd, and equally so in persons and nations. Baseball pitchers or batters reserving the right to judge balls and strikes are not subject to the rules of the game. Violence results when either assumes the right. The nation really observing God's rules also acknowledges a court of competent jurisdiction. Failing to do so it considers itself absolute. The court originally declared competent is God's law represented by organized Christianity. God has the right to impose obligations through the religion He has established; the nation exists to protect the full freedom of individuals to fulfill such obligations.

The nation, now nearly democratic, feels qualified to decide that Christ who is God, cannot be tolerated in the classroom because His presence may embarrass an atheist. It is now American to suppress the acknowledged source of American liberty. Those acknowledging His existence are of course equally embarrassed by His exclusion, but America no longer feels an obligation to protect them. Even the documents acknowledging God as the source of rights must be interpreted to mean the opposite of what they say in order to conform them to prevailing opinion, as is shown in the discussion of private and public schools. It is difficult to understand how a nation competent to curtail even God can feel limited or restricted.

3) In most states judges were once appointed for life or good behavior. They were then concerned primarily with justice rather than popularity because they were relatively impervious to public sentiment. But the slightest restriction contradicts sovereignty, for the distinguishing characteristic of a sovereign is freedom from restraint.

The people are not sovereign while tolerating judges who render decisions contrary to their will. Judges must

CONCLUSION

then be made elective for short terms and reeligible so they become acutely aware of their dependence upon the Sovereign. They are required to bow in all obsequiousness to the majestic multitude and become agencies for the expression of its will. The sovereign which terminates the tenure of judges at his pleasure is not restricted by them. Thus Brownson wrote in 1851 that the independent tenure by which judges originally held office will soon be destroyed in all states.

4) The structure giving existence to man cannot result from his own activity. The source of man's conduct on the contrary is an existence which he receives prior to his own effort. The source of social action is likewise an existing society. Existing social structure cannot be produced by the action of society any more than the individual can produce his own constitution. The existing source of man's social action is given to him prior to his own effort. He cannot give himself a social nature anymore than he can make himself a dog or an angel. An actual social structure rendering social action possible is as old as man and just as indestructible. A population cannot produce its own constitution or unifying factor, but given such a structure men may modify it, just as they may use their power to eat or to commit suicide.

According to our democratic theories a written document resulting from our action constitutes us an existing nation; our consent renders its rule rightful. Thus we view ourselves as self-sufficient, the source of both existence and right. A nation whose conduct stems from this principle must act as though it is God.

The nation is not required to express gratitude because as sovereign it can receive nothing. What it produces redounds to its own glory. Thus we glory in our checks, balances and antagonistic interests, forgetting that if antagonistic interests equal in power exist, government is neither necessary, desirable nor possible. If checks and

CONCLUSION

balances exist and work government cannot govern. They must be made not to work in order to permit the government to act. Our liberty is not then the result of the devices we have produced. The supreme court, the most important institution we established, is not discussed in Brownson's book because it is not distinctively American. Other communities may have both courts and competent judges. Neither gives us a distinctive structure as a nation.

In Brownson's estimation justices of the supreme court ought to be concerned with justice. This means that they cannot act on the principle that their sole function is to determine the real meaning of the laws established by the sovereign people. If this is their primary function justices are either not concerned with justice or they assume that the nation cannot be unjust. Either alternative eliminates right as a reality to which the conduct of the nation must conform. When and if the supreme court decides that the nation is bound only by its own will, the nation is absolute. Then the license to do what it pleases is labeled liberty. An individual is then deprived even of the moral right to complain, because it cannot be right for him to resist right. This is in principle the total subjection of the person to the community.

America of course declared that England abused its power; it made sincere efforts to exercise its own power rightfully. It assumed no right to use its power arbitrarily. It established a judiciary, elevated it above popular sentiment and authorized it to determine how the nation must act in order to act rightfully. The justices of that court cannot determine the rightfulness of the national will without consulting a reality different from it.

The reality the court is required to consult to fulfill its obligations is God's law. But Brownson maintained that the country is so saturated with democracy that no court could consult it and act on the principle of its supremacy in any decision concerning the respective rights

CONCLUSION

of the spiritual and the temporal. The court assumes the independence of the temporal order and therefore its supremacy. It therefore refuses to go beyond the written enactments produced by the nation and the opinions of those whose actions reputedly produced our structure as a nation. They fail to understand the written documents because they view them as supreme and ultimate.

Brownson's thesis then is that a majestic multitude convinced of its absolute supremacy refuses to tolerate institutions which restrain its will. This is socialism. The fashionable remedy prescribed to cure the evil is democracy. This, to use Brownson's figure, is to cure an alcoholic by insisting that he consume alcohol in continually increasing quantities.

In Brownson's treatise the most valuable asset of either the individual or the nation is the structure which renders activity possible. To attribute both man's existence and his power to walk to a wooden leg he has produced is absurd, but no more so than the tendency of the nation to forget about the structure received prior to its own effort. Reliance upon inferior substitutes is unnecessary while its original structure is intact.

Its own structure requires our nation to act through two really different organs called general and particular government. Its political power is not vested in one agent. Since it is never in one place no individual or group however powerful can ever seize all of it and use it to dominate the whole life of the individual. Subservience to God's law is included in the structure itself, thereby rendering concordats with religious leaders unnecessary. This structure enables each of us to keep his personality and to develop to the utmost the powers that make him different from others, yet without danger of anarchy. Checks, balances and antagonistic interests to prevent the abuse of power are unnecessary; government has the full freedom to fulfill it obligation, which is to govern. This structure then

CONCLUSION

represents our most effective barrier against both anarchy and despotism.

Brownson was optimistic enough to hope that Catholic colleges would require their students to understand our institutions; this means knowing them in terms of their origin, nature and purpose. Courses in what he called the machinery of government have no right to the label, political science. He hoped that the men and women who received adequate conceptions in our schools would participate in the affairs of the community; he expected many of them to return to their communities as teachers, and to communicate these ideas to others. He anticipated more conservative trends in politics as soon as Catholics became aware of their obligation to preserve the Republic because it is God's gift. He suggested that they could not fulfill their obligation without increasing the intensity of their devotion to the Holy Ghost.

REFERENCES TO INTRODUCTION

1. Arthur M. Schlesinger, Jr., *Orestes A. Brownson*: *A Pilgrim's Progress*, Boston, 1939; Doran Whalen (Sr. Rose Gertrude Whalen, C.S.C.), *Granite for God's House*, New York, 1941; Theodore Maynard, *Orestes Brownson — Yankee, Radical, Catholic*, New York, 1943. It is helpful to know that these studies are based largely upon a three volume life of Brownson by his son, Henry F. Brownson, who reprints most of the important letters sent and received by his father.: *Orestes A. Brownson's Early Life, Middle Life, Later Life*, Detroit, 1898-1900. It omits purely personal letters, such as those concerning Brownson's quarrels with his family and his indulgence in intoxicating beverages in his old age. Schlesinger's work is perhaps the most helpful, although his treatment of the period immediately prior to Brownson's death appears slightly misleading. The work of Whalen is confessedly pro-Brownson, so much so that it is inaccurate, as is indicated clearly by Wilfred Parsons, S. J., "Brownson, Hecker, and Hewit," *Catholic World*, (1941), CLIII, 396-408. Maynard adds information concerning Brownson's career as a Catholic which is omitted by Schlesinger, and with considerable flourish indicates defects in Whalen's study.
2. His writings which fill twenty large volumes have been collected and arranged by his son, Henry F. Brownson, *The Works of Orestes A. Brownson*, Detroit, 1882-1887. Citations hereafter are to the volume and page of these works.

REFERENCES TO CHAPTER 1

1. The brief account of Brownson's life given in this chapter is based, for the most part, on Brownson's autobiography, the *Convert*, V, 1-200.
2. They did not attend the services of this congregation because its meeting place was too far from their residence. V, 7.
3. V, 4.
4. "Our family library consisted of a Protestant version of the Scriptures, a London edition; Watt's *Psalms* and *Divine Songs*, and *The Franklin Primer*, to which were subsequently added Edwards' *History of Redemption; Davies's Sermons;* a *History of The Indian Wars* by Dr. Sanders . . . , a mutilated copy of *Philip Quarle*, . . . and during the war of 1812 with Great Britain, a weekly newspaper, published in Windsor by Alden Spooner." V, 4-5.
5. V, 5.
6. V, 6. It seems that Brownson gave way to his temper rather frequently, but especially in the heat of an argument. Cf., for example, the following in which Schlesinger, 153, describes Brownson's visits to Brook Farm: "The starry optimism of the dwellers frequently stirred him to debate where, argument failing, he sought to overawe by sheer physical massiveness, raising his voice, pounding on the table, and giving way to anger when his opponents failed to grasp his point."
7. Maynard, 282-283, notes that Brownson was distressed financially at rather frequent intervals. He attributes this not to Brownson's lack of shrewdness in managing finances, but to the fact that they were not sufficiently important to receive a great deal of his time and attention.
8. V, 5.
9. V, 7.
10. The exact extent of Brownson's formal education is unknown. Schlesinger, 7, mentions that ". . . he briefly attended a neighboring academy, probably until his earnings ran out . . ." Brownson says he was attending school at the age of nineteen, but does not indicate his age at enrollment. V, 10. Maynard, 12, n. 13, gives a reasonable explanation: ". . . After Orestes had exhausted his savings, he worked as a printer, and then, having earned enough, resumed his studies." The only thing certain in regard to Brownson's formal education is that it was brief.
11. V, 9.
12. V, 10.
13. Schlesinger, 10-11, notes that his description on this point is exaggerated. He objects, for example, when Brownson says that the members of the Congregation were bound to watch over one another with fraternal affection. Brownson says that "I was not long in discovering that this meant that we were each to be a spy upon the others, and to rebuke, admonish, or report

REFERENCES TO CHAPTER 1

them to the Session. My whole life became constrained. I dared not trust myself in the presence of a church member, to a single spontaneous emotion. I dared not speak in my natural tone of voice, and if I smiled, I expected to be reported." V, 12.

14. The description of his own state of mind may be, and undoubtedly is, accurate, even though it is exaggerated in regard to the particular congregation he joined. It has been noted that Brownson joined the congregation on the spur of the moment. Consequently he was unaware of his incompatibility with Presbyterianism. Furthermore, he was in an extremely disturbed state of mind drawn between rationality or reason and religion. Taking all these factors into consideration one may easily believe that Brownson was rather nervous about the entire situation and consequently speaks the truth when he says that his whole life was constrained.

15. V, 13. Brownson continues the same trend of thought. "This I regarded as unfair treatment. It subjected me to all the disadvantages of authority without any of its advantages. The church demanded that I should treat her as a true mother, while she was free to treat me only as a stepson, or even as a stranger. Be one thing or another, said I; either assume the authority and responsibility of teaching and directing me, or leave me with the responsibility and my freedom. If you have authority from God, avow it, and exercise it. I am all submission. I will hold what you say, and do what you bid. If you have not, then say so, and forbear to call me to an account for differing from you, or disregarding your teachings. Either bind me or loose me. Do not mock me with a freedom which is no freedom, or with an authority which is illusory." V, 13-14.

16. V, 18.
17. V, 19.
18. Brownson does not mention these facts in *The Convert;* he refers to them briefly in XV, 284-285.
19. Brownson became interested in Universalism through his mother's sister who gave him some literature on the subject when he was about fifteen. He had read some of it before he was a Presbyterian. While it aroused his interest it did not convince him. But, after rejecting Presbyterianism, Brownson says ". . . I was necessarily forced back on the point whence it had taken me up, when I believed, so far as I believed anything, the doctrine of Universalism." V, 26. Thus it was quite natural for him to study Universalism more intensely after rejecting Presbyterianism. V, 20-28.
20. V, 30.
21. V, 31.
22. V, 32.
23. V, 38-39.
24. V, 124. The work of John Riedl traces the influence of these men on Brownson in a cursory manner. "The Life and Philosophy of Orestes Brownson," doctoral dissertation, Marquette University, 1930.
25. V, 125-130; I, 215.
26. I, 130-313.
27. The extent to which he accepted these men is still a disputed question. Sidney Raemers, *America's Foremost Philosopher,* Washington, 1931, 17-30.
28. Brownson became familiar with Gioberti subsequently to his conversion to

155

REFERENCES TO CHAPTER 1

Catholicism. Brownson says that he hesitates to refer his readers to Gioberti who is erroneous in many respects, yet he admits Gioberti assisted him in clarifying his own views. I, 241; Raemers, 16, 40.
29. V, 111.
30. V, 114.
31. V, 117.
32. *Boston Quarterly Review,* July, 1840. This essay is not reprinted in his collected works.
33. "If, then, you will have democracy, if you insist on the democratic form, have the courage to go further, and the good sense to adopt the measures necessary to prevent your universal suffrage and eligibility from being a mere sham . . . you must establish and maintain the substantial equality of conditions, so that not merely the *rights* but the mights of men shall be equal." V, 103.
34. On the basis of that essay, Schlesinger, 100, compares him with Marx and says that "Brownson was his nearest forerunner in America."
35. V, 103. "His essay . . . was received as a pronouncement from a leading Democrat. The administration forces, dismayed to find Brownson disrobing in public, had to repudiate him, and to make clear that he was in no way speaking for the party." Schlesinger, 101.
36. ". . . the Whigs reprinted his article and distributed it by the hundreds of thousands to show what it was the President and his party really held." Maynard, 92. He remarks in the same place that Schlesinger has written the best criticism of this aspect of Brownson, Schlesinger, 89-111.
37. XV, 259.
38. Cf., for example, the following: "People, though adopting the democratic principle, told me I went too far, but I knew I was logical." XVIII, 224. "But I can hardly read the essay over without being myself shocked, and wondering at my temerity in publishing it . . . place me where I stood then . . . and I would today repeat and endorse every paragraph and every word I then wrote." V, 104.
39. This point is treated explicitly in Chapter II, 15-19.
40. V. 164.
41. V, 165.
42. V, 166.
43. X, 1-16.
44. Maynard, 160-162, discusses the influence Brownson might have had if he had been allowed to continue to present his arguments in his own terms.
45. Maynard, 152.
46. XIX, 141-142.
47. Maynard, 155.
48. "In 1853, indeed, interest in Brownson was great enough to compel an English edition." Schlesinger, 198.
49. For example, Brownson felt obliged to point out the errors in a work of a very dear friend, George Bancroft. The historian was unable to understand that a harsh review of his work did not mean that Brownson wanted to sever personal relationships. Brownson, in atonement, dedicated his *American Republic* to his "old friend, George Bancroft." XVIII, 1.
50. X, 329.

REFERENCES TO CHAPTER 1

51. XVIII, 404.
52. XVII, 179-210.
53. XVII, 204.
54. XVIII, 204-205.
55. XX, 215-248.
56. XIII, 220-221. His son adds a note saying that this was the most humble passage his father ever wrote.
57. In his *Review* of January, 1844, Brownson is lavish in his praise of Calhoun. Somewhat naively, he closes his discussion by avowing that ". . . we have introduced Mr. Calhoun into our pages, without reference to the fact that he is now before the American people as a prominent candidate for the presidency."
58. XVIII, 1-222.
59. Brownson disclaimed any congenital dislike for the Irish or the Jesuits, though his remarks were unduly harsh.
60. These articles were unsigned. They are included in the collection of his son.
61. XX, 436-438.
62. Maynard, 426.

REFERENCES TO CHAPTER 2

1. "Treatise on Civil Government," cited from Locke, *Selections*, edited by Sterling P. Lamprecht, New York, 1928, 70-71.
2. XVIII, 31.
3. XVIII, 30.
4. XVIII, 30.
5. XVIII, 33.
6. In Brownson's terms, man's activity is confined to the teleological order or the second cycle of creation; his causality, while real, is productive only for the attainment of an end. Consequently he does not originate; he can develop, explicate, combine, but there is no sense in which he can create.
7. XVIII, 33.
8. Brownson mentions, of course, *The Utopia*, or *The Land of Nowhere*, by Thomas More, published in 1516.
9. XVIII, 33.
10. XVIII, 30.
11. "In the state of nature, there is no sovereign; the convention is called for the purpose of creating the sovereignty. But is sovereignty a thing to be created? The sovereign is over and above the individuals to be governed; that to which they owe allegiance; which has the right to command them. Can these individuals create it? Can the creator be subject to the creature; owe allegiance to it; be loyal to it? Obviously, then, if there be in the state a sovereign power at all, it is not created by those who are to be subjected to it." XV, 314.
12. XV, 315.
13. XV, 316; XVIII, 37.
14. XV, 316.
15. XVIII, 38.
16. Cf. Jefferson, *Writings*, (Memorial Edition), Washington, 1905, III, 459: "No society can make a perpetual constitution, or even a perpetual law."
17. XVIII, 35.
18. XVIII, 35.
19. XV, 411-413.

REFERENCES TO CHAPTER 3

1. V, 114.
2. 103-114; X, 33.
3. V, 117.
4. V, 103.
5. Cf., e.g., the following: "People, though adopting the democratic principle, told me I went too far, but I knew I was logical." XVIII, 224. Also, "But I can hardly read the essay over without being myself shocked, and wondering at my temerity in publishing it . . . place me where I stood then . . . and I would today repeat and endorse every paragraph and every word I then wrote." V, 104.
6. XV, 408
7. XV, 409.
8. XVIII, 42; XV, 409.
9. XVIII, 43. The problem is a problem only with reference to a theory which accounts for the origin or institution of government, and is consequently not a problem in relation to nations which are already established under a government.
10. XVIII, 42; XV, 410.
11. XVIII; XV, 411.
12. XV, 339.
13. XV, 339.
14. XV, 321.
15. XV, 439-441; XVIII, 575-576.
16. XV, 414.
17. XVIII, 266; XV, 414. "Now, if the people are, in their own native might and right, the primary and fundamental sovereignty, then, they have the inherent right to command, and, whatever they command, is law; therefore right; and therefore, binding in *fore conscientiae*." XV, 415.
18. CF., e.g., the following: ". . . we put it to our young friends in sober earnest too, whether with them freedom is something positive; or whether they are in the habit of regarding it as merely negative? Do they not look upon liberty merely as freedom from certain restraints or obstacles rather than as positive ability possessed by those who are free?" XV, 272.
19. XV, 5. Brownson wrote this in 1838 two years before the publication of his essay on the laboring classes during the election of 1840. This indicates that his view of democracy has remained substantially the same. His continual berating of democracy after the publication of his essay is therefore a change of emphasis; or rather a change in what it was necessary to emphasize in order to combat evil. Thus the essay and the election crystallized ideas

REFERENCES TO CHAPTER 3

formerly presented vaguely.
20. XV, 439.
21. X, 85.
22. XV, 440-441.
23. XVIII, 42.
24. Brownson's meaning of these terms is clear from the context; they signify the sovereignty of society, the collective people, the state.
25. X, 532.
26. V, 113.
27. V, 114.
28. V, 103.
29. XV, 423.
30. Schlesinger adds, "His flinty intelligence saw how tragically the favorite liberal remedies fell short. Universal suffrage is little better than a mockery where the voters are not socially equal. No matter what party you support, no matter what men you elect, property is always the basis of governmental action." 107-108.
31. XVIII, 185-186.
32. X, 85.
33. X, 85. Brownson does not say explicitly that Italy and Germany will be totalitarian states. He says that social reforms, and he mentions these in Italy and Germany particularly will culminate in absolutism, if unarrested. In XIV, 471, he suggests that the Catholicity of France would save it from absolutism.
34. X, 83.
35. X, 94.
36. "Analyze these reforms and the principles and motives which lead to them, which induce the people in our days to struggle for them, and you will find at the bottom of them all the assumption, that our good lies in the natural order . . ." X, 95.
37. X, 95.
38. X, 93.
39. X, 93-95. Cf. also essay, "Charity and Philanthropy," XIV, 429ff.
40. Cf. the following: "As a protest against an absolute or Caesarist democracy, a democracy which deifies the people — (or a chance majority of them) — if such really existed outside his imagination Brownson's political writings undoubtedly did real service." Maynard, 403. Cf. also Maynard, 181 and the following: "Brownson . . . destroyed an enemy who was hardly more than a figment of his imagination . . . he triumphantly disproves what no sensible man ever doubted." 345.
41. "I am not arguing against a republic, or a government largely popular in its constitution and administration . . ." XVIII, 226. "I repeat, I am not warring against the political constitution of my country, nor am I seeking in any respect to change it; . . ." XVIII, 228.
42. XVIII, 226.
43. XVIII, 226.
44. He opposed it as a radical departure from the inherent nature of our political constitution, which he believed to be a constitutional republic rather

REFERENCES TO CHAPTER 3

than a democracy, Cf. Chapter IX below.
45. XV, 438.
46. XV, 440.
47. XV, 40.
48. XV, 40.
49. XVI, 88.
50. XV, 6.
51. XV, 440-441.
52. "As a rule, men live for their families, especially for their wives and daughters, whom they would see live as well, be as well educated, and as well dressed as the wives and daughters of the better-to-do, whom democracy teaches them to regard as equals." XVIII, 235.
53. XV, 441.
54. XV, 346.

REFERENCES TO CHAPTER 4

1. XVIII, 18-26.
2. XVIII, 19.
3. XVIII, 19.
4. XVIII, 19.
5. This view coincides with an earlier opinion: "I do not regard the family as the germ of the state. It contains elements which are not in the state, and wants elements without which that state could neither be constituted nor preserved. Both in my view, are primary institutions, and neither is secondary; certainly neither is derivable from the other." XV, 325.
6. XVIII, 25.
7. XVIII, 26.
8. XVIII, 26.
9. XVIII, 20.
10. XVIII, 20.
11. XVIII, 21.
12. XVIII, 21.
13. XVIII, 21.
14. "All tribes and nations in which the patriarchal system remains, or is developed without transformation, are barbaric . . . In civilized nations the patriarchal authority is transformed into that of the city or state, that is, of the republic; but in all barbarous nations it retains its private and personal character." XVIII, 22.
15. XVIII, 135, 24. Thus Brownson says that ". . . democrats assert that the elective franchise is a natural right of man, or that it is held by virtue of the fact that the elector is a man, they assert the fundamental principle of barbarism and despotism." XVIII, 24.
16. XVIII, 20.
17. XVIII, 20.
18. XVIII, 22-26.
19. XVIII, 21.
20. XVIII, 21.
21. Brownson does not believe, of course, that states which are republican in principle never abuse their authority. He says, for example, that Rome was in theory, although not always in practice, a republic: "However arbitrary or despotic some of the caesars may have been and certainly were in practice, in principle they were elective, and held their power from the political community . . . The sovereignty vested in the political community, never in the person of the emperor. The emperor represented the state, but never was himself the state." XIII, 110.
22. XIII, 110.

REFERENCES TO CHAPTER 4

23. V, 101. For Brownson's proof for the existence of God, cf. his "Essay in Refutation of Atheism," II, 1, ff.
24. XVIII, 72.
25. ". . . the state is guaranteed against sedition, insurrection, rebellion, revolution, by the elevation of the civic virtues to the rank of religious virtues, and making loyalty a matter of conscience." XVIII, 69.
26. Brownson holds that this is the traditional doctrine of Catholic theologians. XVIII, 55.
27. XVIII, 46.
28. XVI, 69-70, XIII, 492-494.
29. XVI, 70.
30. "Yet, though derived from God only through the people, civil authority still holds from God, and derives its right from Him through another channel than the church or spiritual society, and, therefore, has a right, a sacredness, which the church herself gives not, and must recognize and respect." XVIII, 65-66.
31. Brownson's view of the ideal relationship between the church and state is indicated in Chapter VII wherein he maintains that the American republic is a concrete illustration of the ideal relationship.
32. XVIII, 18-74.
33. XVIII, 18-26.
34. XVIII, 26-40.
35. XVIII, 40-47.
36. XVIII, 47-54.
37. XVIII, 54-58.
38. XVIII, 58-61.
39. XVIII, 61-72.
40. XVIII, 72-74.

REFERENCES TO CHAPTER 5

1. For example, when he was a Platonist Brownson's theories were based largely upon his interpretation of the Platonic theory of ideas; later he based his views partially upon Leroux's doctrine of communion.
2. Inasmuch as Brownson wrote so voluminously on political problems this may seem at first sight to be a statement that is slightly exaggerated. In the first place, however, many of Brownson's views are expressed in rather brief articles, some of which were composed hastily to meet a publisher's deadline. In his *American Republic* Brownson does profess to organize doctrines previously expressed briefly and hurriedly. Still a glance at its table of contents indicates the fact that not one of its fifteen chapters is devoted explicitly to a discussion of the state. He has many chapters on government. In these he discusses the state. These discussions are extremely confusing because Brownson's position demands a sharp distinction between state and government. In the light of his doctrine which follows there is no excuse whatsoever for Brownson to use these terms interchangeably.
3. XVIII, 100.
4. XV, 372.
5. XV, 372-372.
6. "This (humanity) is essentially one and identical in all men, and is to the great body of individual men and women, under the relation I now consider it, what the principle of vitality, or vital force, is to the human body. It is the one vital force in all, the life-current that flows through all individuals, making them all *members* of one living body. It is to establish this fact, that I have insisted on the Platonic doctrine of ideas, and attempted to demonstrate man's existence as an idea or as the *genus,* to speak the language of science." XV, 372.
7. XV, 372.
8. XV, 372.
9. Brownson never modified his conception of society as an organism, although he did modify his Platonism, as is evident from the following, written in 1867: "We confess that we are not able to make out from Plato a complete, coherent, and self-consistent doctrine of ideas." II, 289. His later view is grounded on Leroux's doctrine of communion, which has been stated in a preceding chapter. Presenting his view in terms of this doctrine, Brownson holds that man is a dependent being and cannot exist without God. He depends upon him directly through religion, and indirectly through nature and society. Without society he can neither be born nor sustained in existence. Therefore society is necessary to man and consequently as ". . . inde-

REFERENCES TO CHAPTER 5

structible as human nature itself." V, 131. This is another instance in which Brownson maintains one conclusion consistently but supports it on different grounds.

10. XVIII, 14.
11. XVIII, 15.
12. XVII, 10.
13. XIII, 110.
14. Brownson maintains consistently that the recognition of the fact that the individual is an integer as well as a part of society is due to Christianity. The following is typical of what he holds; "The doctrine of individual freedom before the state is due to the Christian religion, which asserts the dignity and worth of every human soul, the accountability to God of each man for himself . . ." XVIII, 45.
15. XVIII, 15.
16. As is evident Brownson is again criticising the contract theory, that people can get together voluntarily, draw up a written constitution and thus bring a state into existence. This theory has been treated in some detail in a previous chapter.
17. XVIII, 75.
18. XVIII, 80.
19. XIII, 44-46.
20. XIX, 358-360. Brownson also refers to these factors as the Providential Constitution.
21. XIII, 44.
22. XVIII, 81.
23. Cf. *Summa Theol.* 1-2, q. 95, a. 4, c., in which St. Thomas enumerates the various forms of government and indicates briefly the merits of each, and the merits of a combination.
24. XVIII, 97.
25. XVIII, 107.
26. XVIII, 74-75.
27. XVIII, 67-68.
28. XVIII, 72.
29. III, 365.
30. XVIII, 77.
31. In tracing the development of Rome, for example, he says that the "Roman people, had they chosen, could have given a different direction to the developments of their constitution. There was Providence in the course of events, but no fatalism." XVIII, 89.
32. As is evident, Brownson derived this doctrine from Joseph De Maistre, (Anon. trans.), *Essay on the Generative Principle of Political Constitutions*, Boston, 1847. Brownson's review of this essay indicates that he accepted it rather enthusiastically at first. This first discussion is characterized by extremely confusing terminological inexactitudes. While he accepts the terms of the doctrine, such as providential and generated constitutions in his later works, they appear to have an entirely different meaning. He refers to the doctrine rather frequently, e.g., XVII, 494-500, and XVIII, 74-92 where he says that the doctrine is not true as held by that "illustrious Count."

REFERENCES TO CHAPTER 5

33. XVIII, 75.
34. XVIII, 91.
35. XVIII, 105.
36. X, 532-533.
37. III, 338.
38. XVIII, 108.
39. XVIII, 92.
40. XVIII, 92-94.
41. XVIII, 99.
42. XVIII, 99.
43. XVIII, 99.
44. XVIII, 93.
45. Brownson refers to conditions in France in 1848 and subsequently to Napoleon's suppression of the legislative assembly in 1851. XVIII, 93.
46. XVIII, 93.
47. XVI, 538-544.
48. XVI, 545.
49. XVIII, 107.
50. XVIII, 224.
51. XVIII, 107.
52. These conditions are expanded in the following chapter wherein they are applied to a particular situation.
53. XVIII, 106.
54. XVII, 570.

REFERENCES TO CHAPTER 6

1. XVII, 500. His exposition and defense of state rights is contained principally in XVI. He followed, as is evident, the doctrine of Calhoun on this point. His connection with Calhoun is indicated very well in Schlesinger, 114-124.
2. XVII, 486.
3. XVII, 575, 484.
4. XVII, 575, Cf. also XVIII, 125.
5. Cf., for example, the following: "Whether they were justified or not in throwing off the authority of the British crown was a momentous question for them, but is none for us . . ." XVII, 483. Referring to the same revolution he says,"We do not understand how any revolution can be effected by legal authority." XVII, 491.
6. "There is no reason *a priori*, that we know of, why the original British sovereignty could not have inured to the states severally. There was no positive law in force, or legal principle prohibiting it." XVII, 568.
7. XVII, 568.
8. XVII, 573.
9. XVIII, 111.
10. XVII, 485.
11. XVII, 565.
12. XVIII, 109.
13. XVI, 566; XVIII, 109.
14. XVI, 485. The few irregularities probably refer to these instances in which some states attempted to negotiate treaties.
15. XVII, 566-572. Cf. eg., the following: "The political rights of the states hold from or continue the political rights of the colonies while the Union inherits and continues the political rights of sovereignty held by the British Crown, prior to Independence." XVII, 566.
16. XVII, 493; XVIII, 113.
17. "The Articles of Confederation, it is well known, proved a failure, did not meet the wants of the country, and precisely because they left the central government too weak." XVII, 487; XVIII, 113.
18. The following brief passage is cited to illustrate Brownson's argument on this point. ". . . if the English colonies, now the United States, had separately declared and won their independence, they would unquestionably have become separately independent states, each invested by the law of nature with all the rights and powers of a sovereign nation. But they did not do this. They declared and won their independence jointly, and have since existed and exercised sovereignty only as states united, or the United States, that is states sovereign in their union, but not in their separation.

REFERENCES TO CHAPTER 6

This is of itself decisive of the whole question." XVIII, 110.
19. XVIII, 113.
20. XVIII, 116.
21. XVII, 561-563.
22. XVIII, 120.
23. XVIII, 113.
24. XVIII, 127.
25. XV, 558.
26. XVIII, 139-140.

REFERENCES TO CHAPTER 7

1. XVIII, 126-128.
2. XVIII, 189.
3. XVIII, 131.
4. XVIII, 135.
5. XVIII, 139.
6. XVIII, 130.
7. XVIII, 128.
8. XVIII, 128-130.
9. XVII, 484.
10. Brownson himself does not claim originality in regard to this doctrine. He says that he derived it from hints and suggestions in the work of John C. Hurd, *The Law of Freedom and Bondage in the United States*, XVIII, 3. His son, Henry F. Brownson, claims that it is original with Orestes. Maynard, 345, seems to share that opinion. Whatever else may be said, it is certain that Hurd does not present the view as Brownson does. Brownson's constitutional theory, based as it was upon Leroux, Plato, De Maistre, *et al*, represents a synthesis that is definitely his own.
11. XVIII, 152.
12. XVIII, 193.
13. XVIII, 191-194.
14. XVIII, 402.
15. XVIII, 403.
16. XVIII, 178.
17. XVIII, 178.
18. XVIII, 178.
19. XVIII, 184.
20. Writing in 1857 he tells us that in the event of a war between north and south, all other issues would be forgotten: ". . . the party opposed to slavery extension will then, in spite of all that can be said, be an abolition party, and the cry will be 'freedom to the slave' . . . The south can not afford to provoke such a conflict, for in it the moral sense of the civilized world would be with the north, which would be cheered as the champion of freedom." XVII, 65.
21. XVIII, 186.
22. XVIII, 186.
23. XVIII, 189.
24. XV, 204.
25. XVIII, 203-204.
26. XVIII, 205.

REFERENCES TO CHAPTER 7

27. Less than 22 of 222 pages are devoted in the *American Republic* to a discussion of the place of the church in the American system.
28. XVIII, 216.
29. XVIII, 212.
30. XVIII, 217.
31. XVIII, 231.
32. XVIII, 216.
33. XIII, 127-146.
34. XVIII, 217.
35. XVIII, 216.
36. XVIII, 216.
37. XVIII, 217.
38. XVIII, 215.
39. XVIII, 212.
40. XVIII, 218. Brownson believes that the only reason there were rights and duties in feudalism was because the church infused intelligence into civil matters. Such rights were due not to the feudal constitution of society, but to the church. XVIII, 218.
41. XVIII, 16-17; 69.
42. "Catholics are better fitted by their religion to comprehend the real character of the American constitution than any other class of Americans, the moment they study it in the light of their own theology." XVIII, 192.
43. XVIII, 217-219. Brownson concludes this passage optimistically, saying there is nothing in the past history of the country to indicate that it will fail. Some ten years later, however, he indicates his disappointment in the interest of Catholics in political affairs, saying that those who are politicians apparently forget about such factors as honesty, almost as much so as their Protestant brethren. He is disappointed also in their lack of interest in the constitution, which they are well qualified to understand, saying that they know as little about it as Protestants. Even then he is a little optimistic that Catholics will eventually raise the moral standards of parties instead of lowering themselves to party levels. These views appear in October, 1874. October, 1875. XVIII, 562-598. His last article concludes: "Let them (Catholics) study to understand and perform the duties, as well as to understand and claim the rights of American citizens, and all may yet go well." XVIII, 598.

INDEX

Absolutism, 35, 38, 64, 113, see Despotism
Adams, John Quincy, 119-120
Agnosticism, 136, 139-140
American Republic (The), xiv-xv, 17
Anarchy, see Despotism
Aquinas, St. Thomas, 13, 57, 118, 165
"Archbishop Hughes on Slavery," 16
Aristotle, 118
Articles of Confederation, 84, 89-90, 91
Atheism, 142-143, 148
Augustine, St., 13
Authority, 10, 11, 23-27, 29, 32-35, 44, 49-65, 67, 69, 73, 76-78, 80, 85, 96, 101, 106-107, 114, 123, see Sovereignty

Bancroft, George, 156
Baptists, 3
Barbarism, see Despotism
Berkeley, George, 7
Boston Quarterly Review, 8, 9
Brooks, Van Wyck, 13
Brownson, Daphne Augusta, 1
Brownson, Henry F., 153
Brownson, Relief Metcalf, 1
Brownson, Sally Healy, 5, 17
Brownson, Sylvester, 1
Brownson's Quarterly Review, 12, 16, 18

Caesarism, see Socialism, Despotism
Calhoun, John C., xiii-xiv, 17, 83, 167
Catholic World, 17
Catholicism, 12, 13, 14, 107-115, 140
"Catholicity Necessary to Sustain popular Liberty", 13
Centralization, 98, 104, 125, see Socialism
Christianity, 41-43

"Church not a Despotism (The)" 16
Churchill, Winston, 118
Civil Rights, 128-129
Civil War, 17, 82, 103, 104, see Union of States
Clemenceau, Georges B. E., 118
Colonies, 86-88, 119-120, see Revolution
Communism, xi-xiii, 116-117, 136, 146, see Despotism
Communist Manifesto, xii
Constitution, written, 69-70, 78, 81, 84, 86, 88, 91, 92, 94, 98-99, 101, 102, 103, 105, 107, 109,-115, 119, 124, 125, 128, 129-130, 132, 135, 136-137, 140, 142; Amendments to, 129-130; organic or providential, 70, 71, 73, 83, 88, 93, 94, 119-120, 122
Contract theory, 19-30, 69, 84, 141
Convention, 96-97
Convert (The), 4, 7
Cousin, Victor, 7

Declaration of Independence, 19, 84, 119-120, 136
De Maistre, Joseph, 165-169
Democratic Party, 9, 10
Despotism, 35, 50-52, 54, 57, 61-62, 74, 103, 123-124, 146, 152
Divine Right of Kings, 62-63

Education, xi, 135-140
Edwards, Jonathan, 2
Election of 1840, 9, 82
England, see Great Britain
Equality, 9, 31-32, 38-41, 43, 46-48, 53, 103, 121, 131
"Essay on the Laboring Classes". 9, 10, 31

171

INDEX

Federal government, 89, 97, 98, 104, 125, 126-127
Fenwick, Right Rev. Benedict Joseph, 11
Fitzpatrick, Right Rev. John Bernard, 11-12
France, 40, 55, 76, 77, 99, 106, 160
Freedom, see Liberty
Fremont, John C., 17

George, David Lloyd, 118
Germany, 37, 40, 160
Gioberti, Vincenzo, 7-9, 155-156
God, 8, 56-59, 65, 71, 78, 80-81, 105, 111, 124 127, 135, 136, 142-145, 148-151, see Moral Law, Providence
Godwin, William, 7
Gospel Advocate and Impartial Investigator, 5
Great Britain, 19, 76, 77, 80-81, 86-88, 91, 98-99, 106, 150
Greece, 53, 55

Hecker, Isaac, 17
Hobbes, Thomas, 20
Holy Ghost, 152
Hughes,, Archbishop John, 16
Humanitarianism, see Socialism
Humanity, 65-66
Hume, David, 7
Hurd, John C., 169

Imperialism, 99
Income tax, 129-130
India, 76, 78
Individualism, 59
Italy, 37, 40, 160

Jefferson, Thomas, 27
Judiciary, 148-149

Kant, Immanuel, 7
Kefauver Committee, 125

Leroux, Pierre, 7, 8, 169
Liberty, xi, xiv, 10, 17, 26, 36, 57, 58, 60, 61, 63, 72, 74, 95, 106-107, 112, 114, 118, 130-132, 146, 148, 150
Locke, John, 7, 20-21
Lowell, James Russell, xii
Loyalty, see Patriotism

Moral Law, 45, 59, 112, 127, 128, 132,
Maynard, Theodore, xiv-xv, xvi, 14, 153
Methodists, 3
Monarchy, 55
Moral Law, 45, 59, 112, 127, 128, 132, 139, 143
Mott, Lucretia, 15

Natural Law, 57, 61, 62, 63, 72, 78, 81, 112, 113
Natural Order, 114
Natural Right, 31, 34, 53, 104, 107-108, 121
New England Congregationalist, 1

Organic People, 65-66, see Constitution, providential
Orlando, Vittorio E., 118
Owen, Robert Dale, 7

Parochial Schools, see Education
Parsons, Wilfred, S. J., xvi, 153
Patriarchal theory, 49-52, 62, 67
Patriotism, xi, 94, 113, 116-119
Plato, 10, 65-66, 169
Popular Will, 44-47, 123-124, 128
Presbyterianism, 4-6, 8, 155
Protestantism, 15, 111, 138
Proudhon, Pierre J., 41
Providence, 68, 71-72, 94, 95, 115, 121-122
Public schools, see Education

Raemers, Sidney, 155
Reid, Thomas, 7
Res Publica, 52-55, 62, 67, 101, 121-122
Revolution, 60-61, 75, 79, 80, 85, 87, 90, 91
Riedl, John, 155
Rome, 53, 55, 77
Ronge, Johannes, 40

172

INDEX

Roosevelt, Franklin D., 118
Rousseau, Jean-Jacques, 20, 69, 79, 80, 103
Russia, xi

Schlesinger, Arthur, xiv, 153
Secession, 93
Socialism, 35, 37, 38, 40, 41-43, 56, 58, 59, 67, 103, 106, 151
Society, 8, 21-23, 28, 47-48, 66, 84, 106, 112, 121, 147
Sovereignty, 25, 26, 28, 32, 35, 36, 65, 75, 79, 83, 86, 87, 89, 97, 121, 148
Stalin, Joseph, 118
State of nature, 21, 22, 24
Suarez, Francisco, 57
Suffrage, 31, 39, 101-102, 104, 121, 131
Supreme Court, 150

Territory, 29, 33, 34, 35, 53, 55, 73, 79, 100, 105, 122, 131
Totalitarianism, *see* Despotism
Transcendentalists, 7
Trinity, 105-106, 111
Truman, Harry, 118
Tyranny, *see* Despotism

Uniformity, 131, 132, 134
Union of States, 17, 82-95, 100
United Nations, 140
Universalists, 3, 4-7, 155
Utopias, 23-24

Webster, Daniel, xiii-xiv
Whalen, Doran (Sr. Mary Rose Gertrude), xvi, 153
Wilson, Woodrow, 118
World Government, 140-145